THE
ADVENTURIST

Broadway Books

New York

THE ADVENTURIST

My Life in

Dangerous Places

ROBERT YOUNG PELTON

BROADWAY

Designed by Claire Vaccaro

Visit our website at www.broadwaybooks.com

The Library of Congress Cataloging-in-Publication Data
has cataloged the hardcover as:

1. Pelton, Robert Young—Journeys. 2. Travel—Anecdotes. 1. Title
G530.P4173 2000
910'.92—dc21
[B] 99-087243

ISBN 0-7679-0576-8

DEDICATION

Robert E. Lee once said, "It is well that war is so terrible, [or] we would grow so fond of it." I know what Lee meant, for it is in the most extreme of endeavors that the greatness of people emerges. This is what this book is about, and maybe about what happens to those people after their great things are done.

Within this book, there are experiences of great pleasure, great fear, great learning, great insight, and encounters with people who do great things. I never wanted to be plunged into the world of chaos and conflict, but this is where these people are more likely to be found, so it is important for me to go there and return. My journeys have shaped me but I do not seek danger for danger's sake. After all, you should never become too familiar with death, but it is good to keep in touch.

I spend most of my time in the company of my wife, Linda, and my twin daughters, Lisa and Claire. Living simply and in love is a great thing. There could never be a more perfect life or friend for any man. Nevertheless I still leave. To learn and to return again, tougher, stronger, smarter, hopefully wiser. I cannot stay too long in dangerous places or the impressions would deaden me, the lessons would be lost, the contrast would fade to gray.

I am driven by that unexplainable urge I find in all people who strive to do more. This book is dedicated to those who understand and submit to that drive.

—RYP

CONTENTS

ACKNOWLEDGMENTS

I would like to thank the thousands of people who, upon first meeting a gangling, ever-smiling moron, did not just shoot him dead. I thank, too, those who did shoot and missed me. They have allowed this book to be created. I need to thank my wife, Linda, and my twin daughters, Lisa and Claire, for providing the bedrock I build my life on; without them I would live forgotten in some faraway place. This book is a direct result of Eric Simonoff of Janklow & Nesbit, Bill Thomas at Doubleday, and editor Frances Jones, all of whom persevered to bring this tale to the unsuspecting readership.

Some of the chapters in this book have appeared in *Blue, Road and Track, Soldier of Fortune,* and *The World's Most Dangerous Places.* In some instances I have changed or ignored the names of persons to prevent their death or arrest. The other people who have shaped my life appear within.

—RYP
Redondo Beach, California
October 1999

INTRODUCTION

THE WIRE

Life is a journey. I choose to make mine an expedition of discovery, a dangerous one with no scripted ending. If you are still alive to expand your notes, you call it an adventure. If you are foolish enough to hand it off to a publisher, they call it an autobiography.

But with luck and biology willing, I am only halfway through my journey. So let's just call this a collection of short stories once lived, twice told.

At this point it might be appropriate to let you know how I feel about what I have done, to look back and then look forward and somehow wrap it with a ribbon and put it on a shelf. But my life is not like that. My future holds more promise than my past. That said, I would not be looking at the same future without people and events from my past. In the following pages you will meet people I might have been, people who might have been me, and prototypes I have used to model myself. Some have gone the wrong way, some are struggling to maintain their balance, some I have helped, some I have watched fall into the abyss.

At the moment it's like being halfway along a tightrope. I can look up and I can look down. I can look left and I can look right. But it's really about now. Balancing fear and ambition, what I've learned and what I still need to know, where I've been and where I want to go. It hasn't been easy getting here and it would be easy to slip and fall. I have an audience now, curious onlookers who expect more than just a careful progress. They don't see my destination, just short segments of my passage. They make me nervous.

How do I keep my balance? I have connected my passions with my duties, my dreams with my realities, the world outside me with the world inside me. I have dared to cross the line, to search, to fight, to survive, to give, to be an adventurist. This book is an invitation to you to join me on the wire. To take that first step, look forward, fight your fears, to be an adventurist.

INTO A
DEEP DARK PLACE

Redondo Beach, California · The evidence of my past is laid out before me, the record-keeping of my existence embarrassingly incomplete: yellowed jumbo prints, mildewed 8mm reels, stacks of letters, neat rows of vinyl-bound pocket diaries, 35mm slides, cheap drugstore notebooks, floppy disks, newspaper articles, VHS tapes, saved e-mails, digital memory cards, Web events, and wafer-sized ROM chips. Somewhere in there should be a life. My life. The bricks and mortar to support my memory.

My parents appear first as gangly teenagers photographed in wooden poses for slow box cameras. Then glossy photos of marital bliss in faded colors, complete with puppy and kitten in front of cheap fifties-era row houses. I am two going on three.

Then nothing. For ten years.

This absence of record marks a black hole of poverty and indifference. The photos start again when I am thirteen, black-and-white photos of a gangly youth, then a lanky backpacker, the odd professional article on my career in my thirties and then an explosion of media coverage in my forties. An archaeologist might assume that each of these collections describes a different person. Instead they are just four sides of a fortress. Four decades, four lives, four careers, four messages.

The smiling cute kid, the gangly teenager, the success story, the "insane" adventurer . . . all one and the same.

Most people know me in my latest incarnation. If you believe the large pile of press clippings and articles, I am the "tourist with an attitude," "Dangerman," "the Guru of Adventure Travel," "the Real Thing," "the Real Indiana Jones," "Mr. DP," the "Mullah of Mayhem," "the Patron Saint of Adventure Travelers," and even "a man who would make Hemingway appear to be a literary aesthete." In an era where desperate midlife adventuring and armchair voyeurism are in vogue I have become a poster child for the concept of adventure. But only a fool believes what writers are forced to invent. All correct, all wrong.

PART ONE

GENESIS

THE QUESTION

Kabul, Afghanistan · Walking laboriously through minefields to the Taliban's forward line, I pause to catch my breath. The impact of the shells on the gray ground has created white, round scars. But violence is not the strongest impression. Here in the thin mountain air the world seems tired. Wispy clouds float against a light blue sky. Worn, goat-pocked mountains echo not with bleating but with the deep thunder of explosions. The Talibs' most forward position is a ridge littered with large shell casings, unexploded rockets, dug-up antitank mines, and thousands of spent 12.7mm machine-gun shells. Around me is an odd assortment of heavy and light weapons and I am cautioned not to stand up for too long or step off the path. "Mines . . . Snipers," the young black-turbaned mullah reminds me in sparse English. Overhead I can hear bullets whizzing and whistling, short twirps and whines of sound. It's hard to explain how blasé you get about bullets. Like flies that can kill you.

The twenty-three-year-old commander wants to help me carry the heavy and awkward Russian-made field spotters made for looking at the enemy's positions. Up on the ridge about a dozen sunburned fighters are all staring at the new visitor. It can be a little boring up on the lines.

As I crawl up to the ridge with the heavy gunmetal binoculars, my hosts motion me flatter with the palms of their hands. There the high-powered Russian optics reward me with a panoramic view of the flat green plains backdropped by the snowcapped mountains of the Hindu Kush.

The Shomali plains before me are the same ones where Alexander the Great, Genghis Khan, and even the Russians had to rest after coming down the mountains. This battle is not new. The Cyrillic range markers in the spotters remind me that this war has been going ever since I was the same age as the commander. In this incarnation the war is moderate Tajik against orthodox Pashtun. The press will report that it is Talib against Northern Alliance. Southern Pashtuns fighting northern Tajiks for control of an obliterated country. It probably doesn't matter what they write. Not many people follow the war here.

The forces of Massoud below me are guarding the entrance to his mountain stronghold, and the Taliban have conquered every part of Afghanistan except the Valley of Five Lions. It's a source of some amusement to me that I am supposed to be with Massoud's forces and have penetrated into his enemy's territory using a visa signed by his brother in London. I also have a Talib-issued journalist's card in order to get to the front lines. But I am not here to pick sides. I am here to understand this war. When I ask if I can cross over the front lines to meet up with Massoud, the commander laughs, "You can try." The puffs of white smoke in the valley tell me that my chances would not be good. Since the Taliban will not let me cross the lines to meet their enemy, I am stuck as an idle spectator in the company of killers, Talibs who have become my friends and protectors over the last few weeks. Here the fighters have switched from "take my picture and I will kill you" to "take my picture or I will kill you."

Through the green concentric circles of the spotting scope I can see the strategic Bagram airfield about five kilometers away and Massoud's forward lines, only one thousand yards away. The sound of artillery shells flying over my head toward Massoud's lines is invigorating, explosions that smack against my face and echo throughout the valley. I don't need binoculars to see his shells exploding in front of me.

The silence between the explosions is broken by an eerie high wailing. A fighter is standing up with his hands cupped behind his ears. He has a high but strong voice and he is calling the fighters to prayer. Down below, the crew of a Russian-made tank is lining up a shot.

As the call to prayer ends, the shell explodes from the tank in flames and a rolling carpet of dust. And, like a massive punctuation mark, the explosion booms and rolls through the mountain valleys. The shot is accurate and a gray puff of smoke appears on the opposite hill. The tank crew slowly walks up the hill to our position, and casually, as if rehearsed, everyone squats. Asked why, I am told, "We are waiting for return fire." Not wanting to be rude, I sit and wait for the incoming barrage. The return shells hit like a barrage of fireworks, more violent than expected. They are "off the mark *inshallah*" as they say here. Thank God for cheap Iranian shells.

Realizing that Massoud's forces are not going to get any more accurate, the commander invites me for tea in a steel cargo container at the base of the hill.

Despite the pyrotechnics, it really is a wonderful day. Flowers are coming up through the tank tracks and the cool of the mountains is refreshing, but instead of hummingbirds, heavy-caliber bullets fly over our heads as we talk. A fierce longhaired Talib stares at me with interest while he plays with a freshly plucked purple and white crocus. He is quite obviously enjoying the moment and wonders why I will not join them. They all want to hear what it is like on the other side, just over the ridge. They have only seen their enemies as tired prisoners and shattered bodies. My accounts are interrupted by shellfire and dashika rounds, which have a deeper thrum than the smaller rounds. The smaller rounds make a beelike sound. Discussing politics, religion, and purpose with these hard men, I have a sense of clarity. They seek answers in my experience. How can I find such peace in war? How can I not be a Muslim? Why do I not fight with them? I hold my hands in the shape of an open book and reply, "*Ana talib;* I am a student." They nod and smile.

DEAD RECKONING

Edmonton, Alberta · I was born in trivial times. Other generations fought in wars, survived depressions, and made westward treks. I came to be in a time when people were harvesting the benefits of hardship and perseverance. Nineteen fifty-five was the birth date of McDonald's, Disneyland, and *Sputnik*. I came along on July 25. It was a happy time.

I was expected to be Young Wellington Pelton the Fourth. A pretentious first name that would appear to reflect a Yankee heritage but was actually the last name of the doctor who delivered my great-great-grandfather. The family had long ago used up every name in the Bible for their offspring. Peltons were named Preserved, Deliverance, Wealthy, Noble, August, Thankful, Charity, Cyprian, Tom, Dick, and Harry. There are black Peltons, Lutheran Peltons, Jewish Peltons, and even a well-known petty criminal named Pelton Jones. My ancestors made ax handles, sold Fords, fought in every major war from the Revolutionary War to the Korean War. Then they came home and got down to work. They were tall, decent Yankees. If anything, they were renowned for their lack of renown. None seemed to have a burning desire to wander the earth.

My mother's heritage is short-circuited. Named Lynette, she was adopted, cross-eyed, and abandoned in Victoria, B.C. Her last name was Codde and the trail goes cold from there.

My father's father had no formal education but took a bookshelf of correspondence courses in every scientific discipline. My father excelled at mechanical things, winning a scholarship to military college in Victoria. This is where he met the daughter of a socialite at a dress ball at Royal Roads. The tall, stiff, quiet man was in reality a farmer's son and the girl behind the beautiful gown was an adopted and abused girl who desperately wanted to leave home.

Finally, she ran away and my father dropped out of military college to become a salesman for oil drilling supplies in the frozen wasteland that is Edmonton, Alberta. I was the union of their marriage and genetic mingling. A small, yellowed newspaper notice drops out of an envelope. It announces the marriage of the only daughter of Frances and Hugh Parker of Richmond Street to the oldest son of Wells and Frieda Pelton of Luseland, Saskatchewan. The date is what intrigues me. Subtract the date of my birth from my parents' wedding date and it becomes obvious why my parents married. And so I was slipped into the rapidly flowing river that is life. A turbulent life that was to contain an intricate pattern of sights, smells, sounds, senses, and impressions, as delicate as rubbing a daisy on the chin and as violent as a baseball bat to the back of the head.

THE LIZARDS
DO PUSH-UPS

Kani Kombolé, Mali · The heat slams you down like a drunk in a bar fight. It is so hot the color is shattered into shimmering waves that make you blink. In the shade the blue, yellow, and green lizards do nervous push-ups. It is the first time that I am so far out, so alone, in such a dangerous place.

In this godforsaken place a *vieille*, or old man, has taken a liking to me. I feel I am someone from his past and he is someone in my future. He was drafted into the French Army during World War I and was a sailor during World War II. Now he is an old man with little to do. He likes to speak English, but I am trying to better my French. I will learn this hard African French or I will not survive. He invites me to lunch tomorrow to try his fish soup. He was a cook. He has been to Paris. The mud-baked compound is empty except for a white-ash fire and blackened pot. *Potage du poisson.* I enjoy the crunchy bits. When I ask what they are, my host is curious. The soup has been simmering for two days without a lid. They are flies.

For the first time I have found a guide to take me through the horrors. I sit at his feet and listen. There is knowledge beyond books out here.

ENDLESS HORIZONS

Luseland, Saskatchewan · My father's family had a farm in Saskatchewan. A broad-horizoned place where I would jump and tumble in the rivers of soft barley as it cascaded from the thresher into the worn metal truck bed my brother and I rode in. We would get stuck in abandoned cars, drive into town in an old Depression-era pickup truck, and spend a day like an adult with my father's father's father. I would marvel at the massiveness of cows, the depth and texture of mud, ignoring the warnings that my grandmother's brother had once drowned in the lake. I would lie on my back and marvel at the endless pattern of clouds above the flat prairie horizon. I would ride my bicycle toward the white clouds until I was too tired to pedal. My horizon was limited only by personal strength and ambition.

My mother's family was different. They were English. She was adopted. They had dined with the queen. There were doilies on the crisply arranged furniture, and conversation was stiff, formal, and polite. My grandmother made tea in ornate pots that my brother and I were never allowed to touch. My grandfather wore tweed, showed us how to stack the oak firewood, how to fly a kite, and even how to sail a toy wooden sailboat in the waters off Victoria. He was polite and friendly with a soft voice and big hands. The small Tudor home was dark, quiet, neat, and not a place for children.

One day my mother told me that she had been horsewhipped by her mother. I had never seen a horse or a whip but it sounded dramatic. From then on I would sit patiently and stare at my silver-haired grandmother wondering when she would begin whipping my mother.

In my last memory of being a small child I am sitting on two pattern books in our little kitchen when my parents come flying down the hallway, screaming and hitting each other. My brother and I watch and only later begin crying. When my mother asks me why I am crying, I don't know.

GET THE JOB DONE

Coronado, California · There is a naked SEAL dancing on the bar. I keep moving my beer so he doesn't trip over it. There is another SEAL dressed as a gorilla but the girls don't seem to mind. The SEAL sitting next to me wipes up the spilled beer with a bar cloth so the dancing SEAL doesn't slip. It's all about teamwork here. Just another night at Danny's Palm bar in Coronado, California. A few hours ago in the dark part of the dawn SEAL Team Three classmates and I were playing "rescue the hostages" in an abandoned military base about five miles away.

There is some kind of reason for the costumes but it really doesn't matter. What matters is we are having fun.

The SEAL on the bar looks like the lead singer for a boy group: blond, big-toothed, big-chested, thin-hipped, and wholesome beyond manufacture. He used to have clothes on but the dark-skinned girl pulled down his striped flannel pajama bottoms after he did a yippie-yi-kay-yay with his top. He is enjoying himself and the women are enjoying watching him dance. These slightly older women with great, curved bodies and too much makeup are a regular fixture in the long narrow bar. Frog hogs, they call them, usually women bouncing off a bad marriage and looking for some old-fashioned fun.

At forty-three years old I'm not military, Nor am I easy with taking orders, backing causes, or even caring to die on principle. I've never had any desire to fieldstrip a weapon to impress rebels, never wanted to sleep in a dilapidated dorm with hundreds of other men. My worst nightmare would be being sent into combat by a bureaucratic pinhead whose uncle used to be a senator's valet. But I am comfortable with fighters. I have a deep respect for committed people who spend their lives operating some of the most complicated equipment in the world's worst conditions to accomplish the most nebulous military achievements, all at great risk to their own lives.

The blond-haired, Howdy Doody SEAL next to me is a Christian, maybe even one of the Mormons the other SEALs told me about. Mormons are good people, good SEALs, good killers, most of all good operators. People who can get the job done. He joined for peace. He tells me he will be happy never to have to fire a shot in anger. He's here for peace, he says again, the security of our country. I think all he needs is a bicycle, a white shirt, and a thin tie and he could make a fortune selling Bibles to old ladies. He may be here for peace but his teammates seem to have other ideas.

About five SEALs down the bar a very attractive woman is sucking another very attractive woman's right breast. I occupy myself trying to understand the mind-set of another SEAL. The fresh-faced, chiseled lieutenant next to me took history because he wanted to "get into the shit." Much of the language here is pure T-shirt philosophy, or maybe seventies-era war movie dialogue. Here, phrases like "git some," "blow shit up," "kick ass," "mess with the best, die like the rest," and "doom on you" are grammatically and culturally correct.

But SEALs are not stupid, just the opposite. They are hawklike in their intelligence, Buddha-like in controlling anger, and professor-like in their ability to memorize massive amounts of highly technical information. I am flattered that many of these young men have chosen my book on dangerous places as their definition of what life is all about. I never really meet many fans, especially ones that blow things up. They want to come with me on my next trip. I smile.

I feel at home with these men. Clear-eyed, focused men who wait for their moments. Nevertheless there is a difference. They wait for someone else to unleash them. I've never had a leash.

THE KURD

Kota Kinabalu, Borneo · Despite his display of pictures of mutilated people and blood-soaked bodies, what I notice first about Coskun is his eyes. They are soft, humorous, and slightly shy. I am in the Holiday Inn in Kuala Lumpur waiting to start an expedition to Borneo. Coskun has come from Istanbul to cover the event for SIPA press. He has brought his portfolio with him, the equivalent of Granny's brag book but with dead people. Although he is in his early thirties, he has covered all the major and minor wars over the last ten years. The pictures are calculated to shock, to let you know that he is no apprentice or desk hack. "Me in Beirut" he says and points to the book. The picture is of him trying to drag the body of a freshly assassinated politician to safety. The head wound leaves a long smear of blood. Gory, intense, heroic, a perfect calling card.

His physical stature does not indicate what he does for a living. Coskun Aral is short, frumpy, slightly overweight, out of shape, flat-footed, and incessantly polite. He has the usual low-key demeanor of a war photographer, is continuously self-deprecating in his bad English. Despite coming from two very different worlds, we hit it off instantly. Maybe he sees something in me I don't realize.

He started his career when his plane was hijacked in Turkey. He simply asked the Iranian hijackers if he could take their pictures, and despite being beaten and imprisoned as a terrorist after the Turkish military stormed the plane, he earned the respect of editors.

Coskun now makes a living off of death. He is a well-known war photographer for SIPA press in Paris, specializing in covering the dangerous, dirty wars—Lebanon, Afghanistan, Iraq, Liberia, Cambodia, Azerbaijan, and places I couldn't pronounce a few years ago. He is proud of his lengthy incursions into violent places. Despite his herculean efforts to be the only journalist on the scene, his photos are often rushed back to SIPA only to languish unsold. Nobody cares. Then magically one or two will appear in *Time* or another major newsmagazine. Like his shot of millions of Kurds forced into the mountains by the Iraqis. He was there with his own people and suddenly someone cared, his bank account and faith refreshed.

In between wars Coskun covers expeditions. This is my first and I am about to learn that wars and expeditions are very similar. Grandiose ideas that succeed or fail depending on the intensity and will of the participants. Personally I prefer wars, but this expedition will make us the first people to cross Borneo by land.

Coskun and I spend the long days and nights of the expedition chatting about his life and mine. He comes from a well-off family in Siirt, eastern Turkey. His father squandered their money and war made their home unlivable. He moved to Istanbul and studied journalism. What Coskun lacks in technical skill is made up for by his determination to get the shot. For the first time I have found someone seeking adventure for its own sake. He has tried to make a living at it.

THE VESSEL FILLS

Dawson Huts, Edmonton · It's in vogue now to blame things on your parents or society. I don't blame anybody for anything. My early life was interesting and short. Like a cowboy on a bucking bull, I just hung on for the ride. My mother would tell me that my father beat her but I only remember being beaten by her. Once my head went through the kitchen wall. Later my mother would laugh about it when she told people that the place we lived in was so cheap my head went right through the wall.

I never fought back, even when I was crying and shaking and she couldn't beat me any more. Then she would hug me and tell me she loved me. She would clean up the things that were broken and straighten the furniture. It hurt when she hugged me but I always forgave her. When I think back on this time, it still hurts. I know that something inside me broke. I don't blame her—it just happened.

When I was three years old, my mother took us and ran away from my father. One day I had a family, the next day I didn't.

THE BELLY OF THE BEAST

Century City, California · Magazine writers like to give me silly names. I answer their questions for hours, let photographers pose me in silly places, and then they write one page, usually getting half the things I've said jumbled up. They like to compare me with fictional characters, Indiana Jones, Rambo, and other ludicrous inventions. I remind them I am a real person and I find it somewhat insulting to be compared to a cartoon character. It is the realness, the stone-heavy truth, I want them to respect. Anyone can make up adventure. But to seek it, live it, survive it, and make sense of it, now that is real and precious.

A producer from CBS's *48 Hours* catches me on my cell phone and wants to know where I am going next and can they come. I explain that I am heading out on a global journey to visit the world's longest-running war zones. "Great. Which countries?"

Afghanistan, New Sudan, and Bougainville.

"Where's that?"

I explain where and why I am going. I also mention that it might be a little dangerous. I am curious about who will be accompanying me since I know that Dan Rather has spent some time in Afghanistan and earned the nickname "Gunga Dan" for his odd habit of wearing a pistol on his hip.

"Well, I don't know that Dan could afford the dent in his cash flow. Besides, he's kind of busy anchoring the nightly news."

I ascertain that they want to send four, maybe six, people on the trip. When I mention that this might make it difficult to sneak into Bougainville, there is a pause.

"Sneak?"

I explain that we will have to get past the helicopters and navy gunships that patrol the strait between the northern Solomons and Bougainville. The only other problem is the shoot-to-kill order issued by the Bougainville Revolutionary Army for anyone caught trespassing on their island. Actually the shoot-to-kill order was issued by the man I want to visit. There is also the threat of mercenaries coming in to decimate the rebels and, now that I have him going, the very high rate of cerebral malaria and poisonous snakes.

He tells me he'll have to check with their insurance company and get back to me.

I have similar conversations with ABC News, German networks, and even *National Geographic*. They all will get back to me. I can only imagine what they talk about once I leave.

Then at the urging of the talent agency of an energetic agent at ICM a meeting is set up with Fox Television. Fox has become the hip, edgy network by flying directly in the face of television convention and going after a young audience. They have pioneered a new type of reality, shows that are constructed of random clips edited in a frenetic style and narrated by Chicken Little voice-overs that make even the most mundane car accident or animal attack seem like major-league entertainment.

The agent and I meet with a tiny, hyperkinetic man with shaggy hair and cowboy boots. He leaps into his chair and tucks his feet under him like an elf. There is the standard five minutes of trivial banter and then we go straight into the pitch. After a few minutes he gets bored and cuts me off. "Did you bring any tape?" I have never done television but I have brought some clips Coskun shot in Liberia.

The tape shows the street fighting in Liberia. Cranked-up fighters dancing in front of bullets, a young man having his head and then his penis slowly severed by an old man with a machete. Liberia is like that. Fighters from each side will drink, smoke dope, and then start yelling insults at their enemies down the street. Dressed in women's clothing and even butt-naked, they will fire at each other while listening to the sound of American rap music. The victors will cut out and eat the heart of a still-breathing enemy. They say eating the quivering organ transfers power and bravery. They also know the journalists like that stuff.

I am worried that I will gross out my diminutive TV producer friend. He didn't blink an eyelash at the graphic footage and then, bored, turns to us.

"That's nice, really nice . . . that you go to all these war zones and all that. But I want to know what Ma and Pa are thinking just before their plane crashes. What's it like, what are they saying. I want to hear screams . . . something the audience can identify with the next time they go on vacation."

He is essentially asking us if we could put together a tourist snuff movie.

We leave the meeting in a state of silent contemplation. I look at the agent and say, "We have just emerged from the belly of the beast."

Tiny men with Caesar haircuts want to eat me alive.

THE LOAD

Dawson Huts, Edmonton · In kindergarten I was considered incorrigible. My only previous experience was in day care, where I had been entertained by a girl who could shoot bottle caps from between her legs. Nothing sexual, just ergonomically interesting.

My mother worked as a draftsperson for an oil company, and when she took me to the office on weekends, I loved the clear tape, the french curves, the smell of the blueprint machine. My brother and I were not happy until we had jammed up every typewriter, unrolled every tape dispenser, and bent every Rapidograph in the place. There was something exhilarating about writing, drawing, creating structure from nothing.

In my first grade of school I had the dubious distinction of being considered bright but inattentive. In grade two I was considered criminal. I liked to hang out with the "retards" as they were called. The boys with five-o'clock shadows who built birdhouses and chessboards in the portable classroom outside, which seemed like a much more interesting way to spend the day. I learned a lot of things hanging around with these almost adults. I learned that women had at least three holes to boys' one and the meaning of the word "fuck." I wasn't interested in the sex part—just learning about something I didn't know. When I was in class, I would politely disagree with my teacher, mostly about catechism. I just couldn't figure out how they came up with all that far-fetched stuff. She took my earnest questioning as a direct assault on her faith and her ideas of schooling and demanded that I be taken out of her class. After being severely punished I was told I was incorrigible, difficult, and completely unsalvageable.

I was not angry or criminal. If they had looked more closely, they would have discovered that I did not pay attention in grade one because I was reading a battered copy of the *Odyssey*. In grade two my questions about religion were inspired by my readings of Greek and Roman mythology. I even found time to read the entire Hardy Boys series because it seemed much more interesting than Dick and Jane. I just needed to know more than they were telling me. I didn't accept the concept of schooling, assuming it was for the benefit of my classmates, not me. School was where you went because your mother worked and you had to be out of the house.

My mother conferred with Patricia McConway, the Scottish-born, chain-smoking, and heavily brogued principal of the school. It was agreed that I was to be parked in the library surrounded by dusty books until some clear solution could be formulated. A purgatory I relished.

As part of my reformation Ms. McConway arranged for me to be sent up to the University of Alberta to be tested. To get to the bottom of what was "wrong" with me, they fed me a barrage of personality quizzes, IQ tests, and multiple-choice questions. White-coated interviewers grilled me in formal interviews in front of two-way mirrors. They made me stack building blocks, identify ink blobs, and explain why I answered that way. They sent me to talk with counselors, who made notes on yellow pads, and hooked my head up to EKG machines that made thick stacks of folded paper. On Saturdays I had to meet with an academic who patiently wanted to explore my tortured life. I never could understand why he was so interested. Later my mother told me that she stopped the sessions when she found out that he was writing his thesis on me.

Fully expecting some deep physical or emotional trauma to be the source of my dysfunctionality, my mother braced herself for the results. But I had a problem much worse than juvenile delinquency. According to all the scientific data, not only was I perfectly healthy in body and mind but I also had some very precocious talents in the areas of language, spatial relationships, and communication. In short, according to the whitecoats, I should be in university level, not the third grade. The only problem was that I was eight years old, sat in a library all day, and didn't know my multiplication tables yet.

THE LAST PLACE

South of Juba, New Sudan · The heat in the southern Sudan squeezes your head until it hurts. Even the bushes are bent. The red dirt against the painful blue sky plays tricks with your eyes.

Commander Abraham and his bodyguards appear in uniform and the ground around our beat white pickup truck quickly bristles with dusty Kalashnikovs and ragged barefoot soldiers.

Abraham says, "You will see what we do to mercenaries. We leave them to the jackals!" He turns to me, adding like it has some scientific meaning, "But their heads, they are so big. You shall see."

Lanky black gunmen pile into the back of my rented Toyota pickup. I remind them that the springs are tied on with rope and not to load too many. The veterans like to sit in the rear corner. They know what happens when you hit a land mine. Your only hope is to be thrown clear by the blast.

I am just starting to figure out these fighters in the ragged uniforms. The Dinkas are tall and splay-toothed. The Nuers are scarred with stripes and keloid chevrons from cuts gouged into their foreheads when they were young. Their skin is so black it is blue in the cloudless day. They stare at me impassively as we bump and swerve along the bombed-out road.

We are going to see the only monument around here. The remains of an Iraqi group of 250 men who were slaughtered in March. They charged en masse from the base of a hill. The Sudanese Peoples Liberation Army were waiting for them at the top and opened up fire. They finished off the wounded and left them for the jackals. The ones that surrendered were shot.

They always shoot the "volunteers," which is what they call the mercenaries here. The commander tells me that taking prisoners would just invite torture. They were here to die for Allah. "Fucking Arabs" is how the local commissioner described them back at camp. In reality the dead were just naive kids recruited from the *madrassahs*, or religious schools, and sent to fight jihad. Now they are *shahuda*, or martyred, an act that their mullah told them will guarantee them a place in heaven. "We sent them there very quickly," Abraham laughs.

We arrive at a spot at the base of a hill marked by a little sign: "Danger Place of War. 2500 Iraqis Killed Here." I ask if it was 250 or 2,500 and they say, "It was so many." The commander unloads with his detail. He is a former seminarian crisply dressed in American-style green camouflage and carrying a length of cable wrapped with colored wire. Its use is ceremonial but in this part of the Sudan it is also used "to make sure the prisoners understand his point."

Amid all this talk of heaven and hell I remember the fat paperback Bible he keeps on his desk back at HQ. I don't bother to get into a discussion of religious morality.

Pointing to various places on the hill, he explains the battle to me. By now the bodies have rotted and the bones have been picked clean. As he kicks a skull with a hollow clack, he says, "See how big their heads are?"

Some of the Iraqi volunteers were dug in in what looks like shallow stony graves at the bottom of the hill. A number were killed on the ridge, but there were no fortifications or protection in the stony, shalelike graveyard. It was a suicide charge. One Dinka who ran the machine gun said he felt sick just killing them all like that. But he reloaded and kept shooting. He doesn't understand why they chose to die like that.

I hike up the sharp stony hill and find a few bleached skulls and a mishmash of bones. I focus on a pile of bones. There is a white skullcap, a bead necklace, a green toothbrush, and a few strips of clothing. I can almost see the person. The story goes that the Iraqis were making a last-ditch stand to slow down the SPLA. When their commander was killed, they fled. They were then mowed down. Were they attacking or were they running? I don't get an answer. The fighters rearrange the skulls and bones so I can take a picture. They smile and hold up more skulls. One Dinka seems fascinated by the idea that you can still brush the skull's teeth. There will not be any war stories here, just piles of white bones with mismatched grinning skulls. "They fought poorly, they died quickly."

I drive back to Yei with a wounded man, his pet baby monkey, and a few soldiers. The wounded man keeps bumming cigarettes and all the monkey wants is a warm place to hide.

BACKWARD AND FORWARD

Edmonton, Alberta · I followed Ms. McConway around for a few months while homemade remedies ensued. It was agreed that the trauma of being put with adults in university was not wise. Maybe I could be trained to socialize with my peers. Perhaps I could increase my study load. Why not try home schooling? Options were explored and abandoned. I would take correspondence courses, I would sit in the library and read more books, I would follow the principal around some more like a trained chimpanzee and sit in on the various English classes she taught. Finally, faced with spending the rest of my life being either a freak or a teenage doctoral candidate, Ms. McConway suggested to my mother that they begin looking for another way to school me. As I was just entering my ninth year on earth, I didn't really have a hand in my future.

ROCK THE CASBAH

Algiers, Algeria · The gun went off in my hotel while I was strolling through the garden. The old gardener didn't even look up as I sniffed the air for the telltale smell of gunpowder. In Algeria it is best not to be too inquisitive about these things.

The two bombs that went off while I was there were described by the police as "tiny things. Just little transistor toys." The heavy bombs that rocked the casbah were considered warnings, not really attacks.

It all started in Istanbul. Crashed at Coskun Aral's apartment, I was awakened by the phone, an electronic click, and then the *tic-tic-tic* of the fax machine.

It was a crude and rambling fax from the fundamentalists in Algeria. It seems the Armed Islamic Group, or GIA, was doing a little PR work late at night. Most Islamic rebel groups are described as fundamental. With the GIA the accent was on "mental."

They said, "Come to Algeria and we'll slit your throat." Not a "Visit our fine country" sort of tourism intro. The fax went on to say that all singers, artists, journalists, soldiers, and policemen were non-believers and would be killed on sight. It didn't mention travel writers. They had more to say. Belly dancing is a prayer to Satan. "When Satan's messengers give a direction to people, they dance." The fax said that "if you dance, stay out of Algeria." Fine with me since I hadn't worn platforms since the Osmonds were on TV. Maybe this fax was meant for Dick Clark.

A year went by and it started to bug me. Every interviewer's quiver of questions included, "Robert, are there any places you would not go?" So I went.

I went because I told people it was the one place I wouldn't go. I went to see how people live under conditions of fear, and to understand more about the world's most dangerous place. I think I also went to face my own fear, something I have been accused of having none of. I must have fear. So can it be found in the world's most dangerous places? I have written a book that describes in great detail the horrors and dangers that await people, but I have yet to meet them. In each journey I find education, contentment, and strength. I have not seen the rotten face of horror.

Now here I was in Algeria . . . as a tourist. I didn't pick just any time to visit. I chose the most dangerous time. The elections that would finally erase any doubt that the government was truly democratically elected. I descended into this hellish place from a tedious book fair in Frankfurt, Germany. A nice segue, I thought. One day I was consorting with bow-tied, gray-haired intellectuals and schoolmarmish peaceniks. The next day I was descending into the most deadly place on the planet. Usually my fellow publishers at Lonely Planet and Rough Guides wished me luck. This time they just smiled and said, "Isn't that a silly thing to do?"

I shrug off the offer of a security detail at the airport. My excuse is that I am a tourist, not a journalist. They give me a funny look. When I check in at the hotel ringed by the military, the guard also shrugs when he discovers I am by myself. The lobby is a bustling noisy center littered with betacams, canvas briefcases, and journalists lining up for phones and information. The government has printed voluminous books on who's running for what region and there is a long list that must be filled out for the daily bus tours to the various massacre sites. The best trip is the one where they have gunships pounding the forest. Here, the government says, the terrorists are trapped in the forest and are being eliminated. Strangely, no journalist has heard anyone fire back from the lush green hills.

Hanging out on a street corner with some students, I find out the real event here is not the tense elections but the Miss Algeria contest. The students want to know why I am not afraid and I ask them why *they* are not afraid. They say, "Because they will come to kill *you*." I remind them that 99 percent of the deaths in Algeria have been Algerians and they smile and say, "Yes, but they *want* to kill you."

I visit the U.S. Embassy, causing quite a commotion. The golf-shirted security detail keeps its distance from me. A secret service demands and then begs for ID. All I have is an American Express card. They think I want sanctuary. I just want to find out who has been buying Mr. DP T-shirts. The head of security chews me out and then backs off when one of his armed men says, "Don't you know who that is? That's Robert Young Pelton. We have his book in the guardhouse."

I ask them for practical advice about surviving Algeria for my readers.

They say, "Hell, man, we never leave the compound. We read your book to find out what's going on here."

After that, the head of security for the embassy calls the head of security for Algiers. Busted.

That night I am visited by the head of security for Algiers. Mr. Ray Ban, I call him, because he does not give me his name. The U.S. Embassy has expressed its concern that a U.S. citizen is wandering around Algiers. He warns me that I must only go where I am permitted and he will have a detail here in the morning to make sure I comply.

The next day I head straight into the killing zone. The men outside my hotel don't have time to react as I dash out into the street and catch a cab. I have a fair sense of security because most massacres happen at night. There is the danger of fake roadblocks but I have a sense that there will be no "phony" policemen while the journos are here. In fact I am becoming confident that not much of anything is going to happen while the journos are in country. Along the way I stop at a restaurant. The owner is thrilled to have a Western customer, even turns the fountain on for me. He tells me he has not seen a tourist since 1992. I watch a duck swim in a fountain while a cat comes closer to drink. The duck gets nervous and attacks the cat. The cat leaps back. There is also a scabby dog that chases the cat away and drinks at the fountain. I get a bit of insight. The duck is not afraid of the dog, who can easily kill it, because it has scared the cat away. The enemy of my enemy is my friend.

During the day I stop and talk to many Algerians. I like them a lot. They are proud of their land, their history. It is only when you pull out a camera or a notebook that they draw back. All refuse to be photographed. I assume it is because of the terrorists. Later one older man fishing off a pier sees me and says, "Take my picture and talk to me. I am not afraid of the government."

Somewhat stunned by admission that the government is who they fear and not the GIA, I talk to him. He has worked overseas as an engineer in many communist countries. He is used to the black cloak of fear and in his retirement he doesn't give a damn. Even my cabdriver cautions him to watch what he says. My driver also continues to scan the village looking for people who may be overly interested in our presence.

When asked about les affreux—the terrible ones—the old man tells me that the GIA is just one of many problems Algeria has had. "It is like a baby. It is small and weak, then it grows into a teenager, ugly and strong, and then it gets old and dies. And then another is born." He is glad that I am here and that I can see with my own eyes that the people of Algeria are not afraid. I ask him if the West should help. He says this is an Algerian problem and Algerians must fix it. A phrase I will hear again and again.

Back at the heavily guarded journalists' hotel I meet up with an American and a French journalist who suggest we go to dinner.

Their real goal is to interview the person who has now become "the only tourist in Algeria," a story every bored journo wants to file for some much-needed local color. On the way to get a cab, who do I bump into again but Mr. Ray Ban. He politely asks me where I was today. I fudge and say I don't remember the name of the place. He waves his walkie-talkie at me and says, "My friend, today you were lucky. Don't do it again." Mr. Ray Ban is either my nemesis or my guardian angel.

We get into a cab and wait for Mr. Ray Ban to line up an escort for my journo friends. I have never had a police escort, so this should be fun. The experience is kind of like a low-budget roller-coaster ride. You sit politely waiting for takeoff and then the screeching of tires from the police detail lets you know the ride is about to begin. And then you're off, down the twisting, curving streets of Algiers at a ridiculously high speed, hanging on for your life—a nice way to dodge snipers and an ideal way to end up wrapped around a light pole. Our escort consists of four men split between two cars. They wear tight pants, gold chains, and photo vests to hide their pistols and machine guns. They have obviously been trained in executive protection and evasive driving. We careen through the streets at thrill-ride speeds as our escorts swoop, dodge, and swerve. Meanwhile our cabbie, untrained in any method of driving, labors to keep up without being rear-ended or sideswiped by our energetic dodge 'em car escorts.

We arrive at the restaurant. It is closed because the power is out to a large section of the casbah, exactly the scenario that precedes the massacres in the villages. Our guides park in front and behind us, blocking us in and leaving their lights on. I feel nervous. We are well-lit sitting ducks ignored by groups of shouting policemen arguing about which restaurant we should go to next. I wonder if the terrorists up in the casbah behind us are holding their attack, thinking this is too obvious, it must be a setup.

After ten minutes of yelling and walkie-talkieing we are off to another restaurant. Inside is the quaint, colonial, fin de siècle ambience of a Moorish palace. My two women journalist friends interrogate our waiter about politics. I realize this is one of the few times the journalists get to talk to "the man on the street." His opinion of politics is that no one likes the government but that they will win the elections by any means possible. He mumbles this in a low voice while a visible line of sweat appears on his upper lip, then coughs slightly and excuses himself. Our bodyguards may be waiting patiently outside but our waiter knows that this does not mean he is unwatched. As we leave I tell the driver to drop me at the Hotel al-Jezzair and then take the two reporters back to their hotel.

The security guards have a snit. "Can't do it." Why? "We left with three journalists, we must come back with three journalists." I explain I am a tourist and that they actually left with two journalist and one tourist and will come back with two journalists. I will walk.

Confusion reigns. Walkie-talkies crackle. They have never just dropped anyone off before and they have never heard of anyone walking back to the hotel. Mr. Ray Ban comes to the rescue. I hear his voice in French over the radio. "It's that tourist again. Just drop him off."

I now know that I must face my fears. Where are the most dangerous places? In Algeria someone is killing the members of the Algerian press. So far over seventy have died. I head straight for the journalists' compound.

Oddly my driver cruises in past the heavy security. I pick a newspaper office at random. It seems things are serendipitous, for I have chosen the offices of *El Watan*, a newspaper run by Omar Belhouchet, a defiant man who has survived an assassination attempt while picking his daughters up from school. I have dropped in without an appointment, and as I wait in a side office, I rummage through their archives. I learn that journalists are not allowed to wander freely and are forbidden from taking photos unless the military approves it. In many cases the military sanitizes the massacre sites before the journalists are allowed in. A young woman photographer going through some files views me suspiciously. Some photos are ludicrous. A soldier points to a severed finger on a mantel. Dead terrorists are unrecognizable shredded cadavers. Most pictures are of dead people lying in pools of blood. Two photos raise questions. One is of new military equipment, badges, guns, and rifles taken from a bogus checkpoint supposedly manned by the GIA. Another is of a collection of rusty swords, ornate sheep-killing knives, and homemade daggers found at a massacre sight. I am interrupted by the appearance of an interpreter, who answers some preliminary questions.

"Who are the GIA?"

"They are an enigma," she answers. "Nobody knows who they are."

She cautions me against asking the director any political questions.

Belhouchet comes down and answers my pointed questions strongly and without pausing. He tells me he is a journalist because without journalists the people of Algeria would only have the government's point of view. The people would know nothing.

I ask him if having the Western journalists here is good for the image of Algeria. He says the government will not let the foreign journalists into the areas that are really dangerous but they are here only for the benefit of the elections. Normally foreign journalists are not welcomed by the government.

I ask him if the United Nations or other groups should get involved in Algeria's problems. He says Algeria has a history of repulsing outsiders and that Algeria will and must solve its own problems.

I mention that it seems he has become a combatant in this war. He replies that if he has, it is because he is fighting apathy and ignorance.

I ask him who tried to kill him. He says he doesn't know. I ask again if it is the government or the fundamentalists who tried to kill him and he says he does not know. He does not want to forward any suspicions to me and I understand why. He was given a message and he got the point.

As I pack up, the interpreter says, "I thought you said you weren't going to ask any political questions." I say that what we talked about concerned life, death, and freedom.

THE RESURRECTION

Winnipeg, Manitoba, January 31, 1976 · A sixteen-year-old named Ted was training for the annual fifty-mile snowshoe marathon. Like most Saturday runs, he would be out in the afternoon and back after dark, just in time for the chef's chili and cinnamon rolls.

About nine miles into the practice run Ted began to feel the sharp cold that blasts down the Manitoba prairie. By 4:30 it was dark and the icy hand of hypothermia closed around his heart. He was tripping too many times and getting stupid-headed.

About two and half miles from the school he collapsed. Ted's teammates carried him as far as they could and then help arrived in the form of a snowmobile. By this time Ted was as close to being clinically dead as a human can be.

The only person with any medical knowledge was the headmaster's wife, Nancy. She could only try to revive him and vainly apply heat. An ambulance arrived but by then the boy was very dead.

Refusing to accept his grayish pallor and lack of any pulse, the EMS crew continued to massage his heart and breathe air into his lungs as they sped to the Selkirk General Hospital.

Stripped naked on the hospital bed, the young boy's body was lifeless. A heart monitor flat-lined and his internal temperature taken at the rectum was 77°. His heart had not stirred for forty-five minutes.

At this point it would have been easy for a small-town doctor to pull the sheet over the victim's face, but the sight of a sixteen-year-old in perfect health without a mark on his body spurred the doctors to try anything.

They tried a shot of adrenaline into the right jugular vein, then hot towels, then enemas and stomach washes with hot water. Finally, after ninety minutes of working on a patient who had been dead for over three hours, they began preparations to cut open the boy's chest and pour hot water on his heart. Just before they committed to this drastic course they gave him one more adrenaline shot. A small flicker appeared on the heart monitor. Quickly one thousand watts of electricity were blasted through his chest and the heart began a faint, but regular, beat. More drugs like dopamine were injected and fluid was pumped out his lungs. After being clinically dead longer than any human who has regained life, Ted had been brought back.

When I read this story in *Reader's Digest,* I wasn't shocked. It was my school.

SEARCHING FOR THE SEEKERS

Peshawar, Pakistan · My gray-bearded Afghan guide takes me into a quiet corner. He looks me straight in the eye and asks me, "Are you CIA?" I say no.

"Are you a journalist?"

"No."

"Will you make trouble for me?"

"No."

Papa seems satisfied for now.

"Come with me."

We wait until the soldiers at the military checkpoint are occupied with a heavily laden truck, then we walk quickly but purposefully into a compound of shops. Papa smiles conspiratorially and points at the large red letters on a white sign. "No Foreigners Past This Point." After a couple of lefts and rights through the shops we walk through a large gate in the high wall. Just as I'm thinking that this has been far too easy, we turn the corner and run smack into a group of armed men pointing machine guns at us.

Papa pauses briefly. It seems these are some of Afridi's men. A group of about ten out of a hundred heavily armed men who earn about sixty-five dollars a month making sure the drug and contraband business runs nice and smooth. And who should be their long-lost friend and best customer but Papa? Welcomed into their simple barracks, I am introduced to my brigand friends. Not only are the men carrying well-used SKSs and AK-47s but there are machine guns and ammunition cases lying around the wire cots. They thrust weapons into my hands and urge Papa to take pictures of me. They pose with me and bring me tea.

We talk about how to get into Afghanistan and Kabul. Everyone is coming out of Kabul. The Taliban are besieging the city and are poised to attack. I offer to go in in disguise. They laugh and tell me, "You can take the bus right from here for only fifty rupees but there are eight checkpoints from here to Jalalabad and one of them is sure to find you." Another development is that their boss has been asked to get out of Pakistan because of the heat the U.S. government is putting on him. He graciously has moved out of his compound to another one high in the hills of Jalalabad. He is not about to get into more trouble by inviting some foreigner for dinner and a ride into Kabul. Although his bodyguards are eager, they know I'll be arrested and turned back. They also explain that the Taliban execute drug dealers and it might not be wise for me to arrive under their protection. It looks like the Khyber is not the way to go.

Papa shows me around the market where piles of sickly-looking hashish and heroin are on display. There are also piles of well-used weapons and even lethal pen-guns that fire one bullet. The merchants watch me with some remorse as I jot down the going rates. Two kilos of hash goes for $170, ten grams is $2.50, one gram of injection heroin is $3, and one gram of smoking heroin is $1.50. In this market weapons are to drugs as shovels are to farming. I can pick up a slightly used rocket launcher for $1,000 (rockets are $13 each), a hand grenade for $3, a Russian AK for $200, a beat-up AK-47 for $250, a "short" Chinese-made assault version of the Kalashnikov for double that, and thirty bullets go for $10. A helpful salesman reminds me that the barrel of the Chinese AK doesn't get as hot as the home-made version. I nod with authority.

Papa says he does a little bit of this and that to make ends meet. Besides drugs (he prefers to buy his drugs directly in Afghanistan, in the region of Mazar-e Sharif), he also buys stamps for stamp collectors and takes the occasional tourist around Peshawar, but mostly he directs foreigners to where they can buy drugs. I tell him that I would like to look around the northern border areas until I can figure out how to get into Afghanistan. I ask him if he wants to go visit the remote mountain areas of Gilgit and the Kalash Valley in Pakistan and he agrees.

I thought I traveled light, but Papa puts me to shame. The next morning he is carrying all his travel gear in a tiny plastic sack. We take the postal bus north to Mingora. On the bus he casually mentions that the bodyguards we met yesterday were asked by the Pakistani police to help show the United States that they were cracking down on drugs, so Afridi's bodyguards offered Papa $350 to bring them people to turn over to the police. I ask him if he would have set me up. He smiles in a hurt way and says, "But you are my friend."

Afghans are a complex result of their code of honor. If you become their friend, they will deny you nothing. Pathans hate haggling or coyness and are much happier when you simply state your purpose no matter how far from the legal path it strays. Get on the wrong side of a Pathan and he will kill you for even the slightest wrong.

Along the way we talk about many things. Papa is amazed at the strange places I have been, and I am equally intrigued with his stories about his home in Afghanistan. He grew up in a small town along the Khyber Pass in a fortresslike house where the only profession was smuggling. Every member of the family had to post guard duty in the tower and every house was heavily armed. They fought over goats, women, past wrongs, and anything else they found worth killing for. Many villages and clans have been warring for years simply because every new generation must carry on the revenge, or *badal*, for the continuing seesaw of bloodshed.

It is October and as we climb higher and higher into the mountains, we are getting cold. Now I know why Papa didn't bring any clothes. He is determined to get mine. He compliments my black Goretex jacket through shivering teeth. He praises Allah for creating such a marvelous garment. Knowing full well that it is a custom to give something that is so lavishly praised as a gift, I say, "No, Papa, you can't have it." Finally I give it to him. Damn these wily Pathans.

Back on the road in the back of a battered Toyota pickup truck I rented, we bump up the mountain pass. I ask Papa how old he is. He tells me that only rich people pay attention to things written on paper. I tell him I like to cook. He tells me that is women's work, he has no idea how to cook. I jokingly tell him that he would starve if he did not have a woman to cook for him. "I cook tea," he replies indignantly.

I show Papa pictures of my family. Seeing the pictures of my twin daughters, he compliments them profusely. He exclaims, "I must have these for the chief of the Kyhber's son. He is a fine man and his father feeds fifty people a day!" I look at my jacket and shake my head. I don't know how I will break the news to my daughters that they have both been betrothed to one of the world's largest drug smugglers. I put away the pictures before he can compliment them too much.

THE HAMMER

Winnipeg, Manitoba · Despite its august religious name, St. John's was an unusual school, founded in Winnipeg in 1957 by a German Canadian named Frank Wiens, who believed that public schools didn't get the best out of students. One of Wiens's first missions was to enroll a bunch of kids to push around old rowing cutters on Lake Winnipeg in an effort to reprise a long-gone method of transport. Ideally this would teach the kids how to overcome obstacles and instill values they believed were lost: hard work, perseverance, etc. When cutters proved too difficult, St. John's graduated to large freighter canoes. In an ancient stone house north of Winnipeg, and with the help of St. John's Cathedral and church volunteers, the school formed the Company of the Cross. Then this religious group sought volunteers in the manner of the ancient Jesuit tradition, or even the Company of Adventurers. A typical recruitment ad for teachers read:

TEACHER TRAINEES

For the toughest boys' school in North America
Would you be willing:

- to learn to teach in the traditional manner in a highly disciplined setting where the major goal is to teach boys to think?
- to paddle thousands of miles, snowshoe up to fifty miles at a time and run dog teams throughout the north country?
- to rise at 6 a.m. and work until late at night?
- to work the garbage detail or clean the chicken barn?

- to face your own weaknesses and overcome them?
- to examine the Christian faith as it relates to you personally?
- to do this for only $1 a day, room, board, and living essentials?

As you can imagine, this type of approach can attract the best and worst in teacher material.

The entire budget of the school was $115,000 and the expenditures were supposed to be about $103,000. Each student was supposed to pay about $800 and then buy clothing and sports gear: about $60 for durable clothes and maybe a few bucks for a lacrosse stick.

The school was set up to be a self-sustaining Christian boys' school with an intensive physical and mental curriculum. Students were expected not only to attend a full day of classes but to build, maintain, repair, and support the school. We also did the mundane chores of cooking and cleaning. In addition to attending chapel and church on Sunday and somewhere in between mandatory homework sessions at night, we raised chickens and pigs, butchering them and then selling the end product door-to-door. Although when all was said and done the school discovered they didn't make money at this carnal pursuit, it kept us busy.

THE STUDENTS

Peshawar, Pakistan · I have been told that the Taliban will kill foreigners, that they are very strong and hate the West. I hear a lot while I am in Pakistan trying to sneak into Afghanistan. When I hear they have a headquarters in the Afghan market, I go back to the hotel to get Papa. Papa is not pleased. It seems that he heard me just fine when I asked him about the Taliban before. That's why we magically never found them in our wanderings over the past two weeks.

Now Papa has lost his joviality, he is dead serious. "You understand that we are going to a place where they can kill you?"

"Yes, but I don't think they will."

"Do you realize we are going to a place where they may kill me?"

"Then don't go."

"I cannot let you go alone because then they will kill you and I will be to blame."

"Then come and we will visit the fighters."

I grab my cameras and we jump on a bus and I am elated. Papa is quiet.

As I stride past the money changers in the market, we ask where the office of the Taliban is. The men point in a general direction but do not take us there.

As we come across the tracks of the train that goes into Afghanistan, the muezzin calls the people to prayer. "It is time for me to pray," Papa says. "Please wait here."

Plunking myself down in the shade, I notice two sun-browned men with black turbans sitting eating in the open. Black turbans with long tails and white stripes—the symbol of the religious student. I can't believe how blind I've been—this is the uniform of the feared Taliban. I nod in their direction and they stare back grimly.

Papa comes from washing up and praying and nods toward the fighters. "Taliban."

I wave as I walk by and ask if I should take their picture. Papa says, "Please, no." I notice that besides prayer, Papa has fortified himself with hashish.

A young boy directs us to a nondescript house with heavy green metal gates. Outside, two men with machine guns sit in the shade. Walking past the men, I push through the lower half of the gates. I startle a man behind the gate. I am staring into a face from the first century. The man is dressed in white robes with a white turban. His eyes are piercing and ringed with *kohl,* a black eyeliner, which rural Afghanis use to keep evil souls from entering their eyes. Behind him is a group of men with vicious wounds, some with missing legs, others with gashes and bandages. They sit on a pile of dirty blankets three or four feet high. Papa is about eight feet behind me and I motion him forward to make the introductions.

In the courtyard I walk past a battered ambulance and the Taliban's troop carrier of choice, a well-used white Toyota pickup truck. Black headdresses are hung up to dry. They are over twenty feet long and look like odd mourning flags hanging horizontally in the sun. There are wounded men lining the staircase. At the head of the stairs I take off my hiking boots. They look massive and odd in the pile of dusty cheap sandals. At the door I am met by a young man named Abdul Ghafoor Afghani. He is twenty-three and when asked for his title calls himself the "information person." We are taken into a dingy green room to wait. Sitting on a scabby yellow and red plastic mat, we take in our surroundings. A ceiling fan is motionless. There is no electricity but the light switches are grubby from many hands.

In various other rooms are badly dressed, turbaned men in *shalwars* who huddle in deep discussions. By the hard brown look of their hands and faces I guess many of them are farmers, not soldiers. Abdul, our host, invites us into the main room to chat with the leader. He is wearing the white turban of the mullah and a fully packed bandolier containing an ancient revolver. He looks a little pissed at us for interrupting his meetings. He asks Abdul to apologize for the pistol, but the market is a stronghold of Hekmatyar, the leader of Hezb-i-Islami, and somebody tried to assassinate him yesterday. He is wearing it just in case they try it again.

He apologizes for having no "propaganda" to give me, but, he says, the Taliban is still in its formative stages, is only a year old. "What is their mission?" I ask.

"We the Taliban wish to rid Afghanistan of robbers, rapists, killers, and militia and to create a new Islamic country." He tells stories of how the movement started in October 1994. In Kandahar there was a brutal warlord who stopped everyone at roadblocks along the border with Pakistan. His men forced these stopped drivers to put on makeup, sodomized and then killed them. The people were infuriated but could do nothing. The religious students, or Taliban, rallied the people at the mosque, got the people together, and hung the leader and the gunmen from the barrels of their tanks. From that point on, the revolution was in motion. They have not met many Westerners. So far, the British have sent in a BBC crew and an independent TV crew but that is it. I am the first person from North America they have met.

I ask him if I can journey to Kandahar and the front lines or send in a film crew to interview the leaders and cover the war. He would like that. I ask him again, to make sure he is not just being polite. There is one catch—the leaders of the Taliban do not allow their photographs to be taken because of the Koran. I explain very carefully that only cowards do not show their faces and that in my culture a man who does not wish to be seen cannot be trusted. Just to make sure I get my point across I ask, "Must their leader hide as women must hide behind the veil?"

This gets the calculated result. There is silence in the room. To break the tension my young host invites me to share lunch with some fighters that are assembling outside the door. I sit down to a simple meal of red beans and flat bread. I am amazed at being in a place where a group of ragtag students is taking over a country. But it is not that simple. As we share lunch, it is obvious that he is hoping to convince me that they are sincere in their goal. He does not understand why I ask some of the questions. I tell him that it helps me understand the world better and hopefully I can help other people understand as well. Some fighters that have joined us insist that I finish the last of the watery broth as a courtesy. It is a humbling experience.

After lunch Abdul, not knowing what he should do with his visitor, offers to show me around the cluttered cramped compound. He says I cannot take pictures of the men upstairs but that maybe the men downstairs won't mind. He explains they had trouble before with the Russians using pictures to identify and kill people. Downstairs the men are lounging on grubby blankets, recovering from various war injuries. As I lift my camera, a man with a deep face wound begins swearing at me. He says that Allah does not like photographs and that I should get a better job than being a thief. I click away while Abdul and Papa get nervous. Trying to ease the tension, I ask Abdul to take my picture. He holds the camera backward, the lens facing his nose.

The haranguing continues as I tour the compound. I point to the black clothing and ask Abdul if this is the uniform of the Taliban. He laughs and points to all the men and says, "He is Taliban, he is Taliban, and he is Taliban. We do not have a uniform."

He excuses himself and I thank him for his time. I remind him that I will be sending in a film crew. He says of course, we shall do what we can.

Out in the bright light of the market, people stare at me. I have my picture taken by an old man with an ancient wooden camera. A crowd of Afghans press around me. Someone plunks a *pakool*, an Afghan cap popular in Nuristan, on my head. He uses the lens cap as a shutter and then develops the paper negative inside the camera. He then photographs the negative to give me a blurred two-inch paper portrait. When he hands me the crude, orthochromatic picture, I am surprised. I am looking at a pale-eyed Afghan from the eighteenth century. I am in a time machine and I am holding the proof in my hand.

I sit in the shade while Papa goes to pray in the simple mosque across the tracks. While I wait a Talib fighter comes up to me to practice his English. We watch a young boy walking around with a white plastic garbage bag and a handful of wooden splinters and sticks. My new friend sees me looking at the young boy and says, "He does this every day. He will take these things and make a beautiful kite."

That night in the hotel I call Coskun in Istanbul and tell him that we can have the world's first filmed interview of the Taliban leaders, that they will meet and pass a special *fatwa* for us to allow us to film them. I tell Coskun of the route I have set up and give him my contact's name. He thinks I'm crazy but he says he will be here as soon as he can.

THE DEAD

Lake Temmiskaming, Ontario, June 11, 1978 · Something had gone wrong, terribly wrong, on a canoe trip in northern Ontario. Something about a survival school or religious school, the media couldn't quite make up their minds, but something very awful had been discovered floating in a frigid lake. I was not there but I had been there many, many times.

The four canoes had pushed into the cold water of Lake Temmiskaming early Sunday morning. The long lake was calm when they started and the June trip was going to follow the route the Chevalier de Troyes took in 1686. The twenty-seven boys and teachers hadn't come this way before, but they had read the account of this journey in history books and now they were re-creating it. It was part of the curriculum of the school; you learn by doing.

One of the steersmen had never been on a canoe trip of this nature but the other steersmen, though young, were seasoned. It would be tough, but things had always turned out fine. The boys (the youngest was ten) looked eager and fresh on this first day of the canoe trip that was to last three weeks. Locals knew that the eighty-five-mile-long lake could turn ugly.

The next day a helicopter pilot was flying over the lake and thought he saw something floating in the water, small white bodies in orange life preservers and an overturned blue canoe. He radioed for help and soon volunteers came from across the lake in boats to pull the lifeless bodies out of the frigid lake. When it was done, there were thirteen bodies: twelve children and one adult.

The press flew in and the coroner began an investigation. The press was abuzz about troubled kids, potential dropouts, under-achievers, boys who do not fit in the regular system, religious train-ing, survival schools, and other labels. The journalists were trying to find out how this could have happened. The sight of the pitiful white bodies led the locals to ask: how could all these young children be out on a lake without a radio, rescue training, a backup plan, or any means of rescue? The emotionally shattered parents, teachers, and surviving students kept up a brave face but they had no answer.

The incident on Lake Temmiskaming still stands as the worst boating accident in Canadian, and possibly North American, history, and when it was all over, the coroner described it as "an exaggerated and pointless adventure."

I kept the clippings on the disaster in a drawer. Then one day I was rummaging through the pile of clippings and came across an older piece on the school in a weekend magazine. The large headline? "The Toughest Boys School in North America." Maybe it was.

THE LOST WORLD

Maliau Basin, Sabah, Malaysia · The helicopter pilot tapped his gauge, alerting me to his low fuel. I broke out of my aerial reverie and began to search for a place to land. We had flown over miles and miles of green undulating jungle of Borneo, a thick, mist-streaked carpet bro-

ken only by brown mud-swollen rivers that snaked like Chinese dragons. If we went down, no one would find us. The pilot was anxious
to get back.

Now we hovered over the object of my expedition, the crisp shape
of a clouded continent thrust above an ocean of jungle. The sharp
outline of the limestone cliffs cut an exact shoreline in the cloud. No
one had penetrated this massive remote interior. Until now.

We began to sink down from the icy skies to the close heat of the
jungle below. Even when we cleared the tops of trees, we were still
three hundred feet from the ground. The Bell 206 Jet Ranger touched
down lightly in a narrow clearing, not really putting any weight on
the undergrowth. I leaped out and immediately sank up to my chest
in moss. The firm peat forest floor was an illusion. There were three
to four feet of moss and leaf litter before the trees rooted in the thin
hard bedrock below.

Laboring like horses in deep snow, my team moved the gear away
from the rotor wash. As the chopper lifted back into the bright sunlight, we had a chance to record our first impressions of the Maliau
Basin, the Lost World.

I looked around at my group: Coskun, guide Jon Rees, and
botanist Tony Lamb. Four people in a place with no maps, no charts,
no history—a newly discovered place. I sent Coskun and Jon with
our gear to find a campsite lower down and we agreed that Tony and
I would follow the rim and meet them later that day. In retrospect, a
stupid mistake. In the exhilaration of the moment, however, fresh
from the whine of turbines and the descent into this pristine place, I
wanted to explore without a crowd following me.

The curious lack of soil and the depth of the moss were typical of
a peat forest. The trees were not the usual lowland dipterocarps of the
jungle below. Here, there were conifers. Big conifers. And after the
bup-bup of the Jet Ranger faded away, silence.

From high above, the Maliau Basin looks like an elephant track in
hard dirt that has been washed by rain. But from down below, it is a

crown shape that rises in the north to a tiara-like configuration and slopes down on each side to rivers that have cut a series of jagged canyons through which they spill like wax from a candle. An important drainage basin, the Maliau is easy to spot on aviation maps and satellite photos if you look just below the northeast corner of Borneo. This basin creates the Maliau River, which tumbles down to create Maliau Falls, then drains into the Kuamut, which links up with the Kinabatangan and drains into the Sulu Sea.

Within this chain are rapids and waterfalls that spill over house-sized boulders, cascade twenty to thirty feet, then pool to create still more basins—an extraordinary sight. Now, however, I could see nothing but massive trees. The soft contours of the basin, which had seemed to rise gently from the center, were now wickedly steep and forbidding chasms. The forest, which had seemed green and benign, was a set for a horror film, with wet moss hanging off branches and the eerie silence of a graveyard. As soon as we left the clearing, we were plunged into a dull dark world. Slowly we began to climb over logs and make our way in the pathless wilderness.

Five minutes later Tony had already made a discovery. Pointing to a thimble-sized plant that resembled a cross between an alien space-ship and a Victorian lamppost, he proudly announced the second-ever discovery of a small saprophytic plant, *Thysmia aescananthus*. I was about to step on it.

I had arrived filthy, sunburned, mud-dirty, and disheveled, fresh from exploring giant caves in the interior of Borneo, shooting rapids, sliding through dark forest floors, and being knee-high in cockroach-filled bat shit.

Having spent the late eighties doing expeditions to places no one had ever been to before, I was eager to see what the last wild places looked like. Having worked in the forest in the Yukon and British Columbia for the forest service in my youth, I felt an urge to see more of these special places before they disappeared. Back in California I had an entire office of people, complete with clamoring clients and organized mayhem, a whole other world to worry about. Borneo was a day of flying, a day lost crossing the time zone, and then another day of flying from mainland Malaysia, and then another day to get into the bush. By the time I arrived I didn't even know what day it was. After two weeks of hard travel in the jungle I didn't even know what century it was. Here away from the strange rituals and stress of business, things were simple, momentary, and direct. I loved it.

Tony patiently explained to me that we were in unique coniferous forest dominated by huge *Agathis* (related to the New Zealand kauri pines), *Dacrydium*, and *Podocarpus* trees, along with oaks and casserinas, as they mix with the lower-hill dipterocarp forest. All I knew was that there was forest in every direction and I was using a bad copy of a hand-drawn map to navigate.

This area got its nickname, the Lost World, back in 1947, after a pilot flying from the capital of British North Borneo to Tawau experienced a rude shock when he narrowly avoided colliding with a wall of steep cliffs emerging from the misty jungle. This incident is the first recorded mention of the headwaters of the Maliau. The area was known by the local headhunters but Dusun villagers, who lived four days away, kept away from the summit as they believed a fierce dragon inhabited Lake Limunsut at the base of the cliffs. Muruts along the Sapulot River were known to have reached the lower basin, calling it the Mountain of Stairs in reference to the many waterfalls and limestone ledges, but no one had dared attempt the steep cliffs and house-sized boulders that protected the mysterious, cloud-shrouded top. The first Western attempt to enter the Lost World was in 1976 during a forest service expedition to Lake Limunsut. After trying in vain to scale the escarpment they were forced to turn back just forty feet from the upper edge. Four years later the Sabah Museum mounted an expedition to penetrate this remote area. But that expedition ran out of supplies, was felled by malaria, and had to give up before they could try to conquer the escarpment.

In 1982 a joint military and scientific expedition sponsored by the Malaysian government managed a brief reconnaissance by helicopter, landing on a gravel bar near the falls. This preliminary mission was designed to lay the groundwork for a more intensive expedition a year later. Landing, they were greeted by animals that had never seen man before: a docile twenty-two-foot, four-hundred-pound python, mildly curious bearded pigs, and a *kijang* deer. Then, in April–May of 1988, a forty-three-man expedition spent three weeks in the lower part of the Maliau Basin trying to unlock its secrets. What they found was impressive. The 390-square-kilometer basin is 25 kilometers across and is protected by an encircling escarpment that climbs up to 1,500 meters. The highest point is Gunung Lotung, estimated to be 1,900 meters high, but it has yet to be properly surveyed.

This expedition identified 47 species of mammals, including the very rare Asian two-horned rhino, proboscis monkeys, and clouded leopards; 175 species of birds, including the Bulwer's pheasant (once thought extinct in Sabah); and 450 species of plants, many of them rare. The scientific finds and increased understanding of this absolutely untouched region led the government of Malaysia to propose the region as a conservation area. They were also worried about the impact of something else they found. Along with the numerous rare plant and unusual ecosystems, the expedition discovered significant, sulfur-free coal seams.

I was here because I had heard that despite the area's potential for scientific discovery, there was a very real danger of the region becoming an open-pit coal mine. I was determined to bring attention to the region and had brought the help of someone who could verify the importance of the region.

Tony Lamb was a botanist known for his work in the identification, propagation, and domestication of tropical fruits. He had set up the Tenom Research Center in Sabah for testing the viability of every possible type of plant for cultivation and future preservation. He had created a land-based Noah's ark. He also had a vast knowledge of Borneo's insects, birds, and mammals; his knowledge of the orchids and plants was encyclopedic. Tony was born in Ceylon (now Sri Lanka) and grew up on a tea plantation during the British colonial period. Education in England and many years in Malaysia, another former British colony, explained his genteel and patient nature.

My idea was to penetrate the upper, unexplored reaches of the Maliau and then head into parts unknown. To get there, we would follow the very edge of the rim, then cut down along the other side of our rendezvous at a prearranged base camp. The distance on my soggy, hastily drawn map hadn't seemed like much, but now that we were down on the ground we felt like ants on a lawn.

We could tell when we were close to the rim when we hit a green wall of moss. There is a distinct rim forest that lives in the constant wash of the mist and fog that pour over the rim. There the trees are twisted and gnarled, their roots raised as if to keep their feet dry. "Sea" is an appropriate description because the mist bobs and ebbs like an ocean. It hits the cliffs, curls up, and then floats above the trees, spraying a fine cool mist over the trees and moss.

Searching for the rim, I discover that the spectacular view I thought would greet me does not exist. The dense growth blocks any chance to get a clear view of the surrounding jungle below. When I push out to get a view over the ledge, I have a gut-wrenching revelation. When the mist clears for a few seconds, through the holes in the roots I can see a thousand feet straight down. The limestone cliffs are behind me.

Wiser, I gently return to the safety of the cliff five feet behind me.

It has taken us a long time to get this far and the day is getting late but based on my calculations and crude map, we are still quite a long way to camp. Looking back, I can see the profile of the cliff that matches the map. The problem is I am looking up at the ridge and it is behind me.

As all lost souls do, we continue without changing course. We really can't do much else, though, as we have found a narrow pig trail that is easier to negotiate than crashing through virgin forest. The trouble is we are losing altitude at an alarming rate. Now I am sure something is wrong. The map shows a smaller plateau below the cliff edge. We have been mindlessly following a game trail that we assumed would follow the ridge. Instead, we have found a way out of the basin and down the cliff. That is good news and bad news. The good news is no one has ever discovered a way up to the ridge from down below. The bad news is that we are completely off the map.

We discuss our situation. We could turn back, but we don't know exactly where we went off the ridge and down onto this lower plateau. Since the path winds and curves tree by tree, there would be no sure way of knowing where the path diverged, if it diverged at all. Plus, it is getting darker. Being lost at night with sheer cliffs around is not a welcome feeling.

We decide to go forward because it will take us closer to our rendezvous. We will then cut in toward the cliff face as we get to the end of this minor plateau. There might be a way up, similar to the way we were fooled into coming down.

We continue losing height until we are in the depths of a black swamp. Trees block the light as our feet are sucked into the dark ooze. Noxious gases are released as we struggle to pull our feet free. A blue oily film floats on the surface of the mosquito-infested slime. We have gone from bad to worse.

We decide this is not the place we want to spend our first evening. Looking at the cliffs looming above us, we make a bold decision. We will push up the cliffs, since the path we are taking goes deeper and deeper into the lowland jungle.

Tony is tired. He has been helicoptered in from his comfortable desk job and is now sitting in a dark swamp, about to cliff-climb with a stranger, at night, in one of the most remote jungles in the world.

I am concerned about him. He has twenty years on me, but he is the one who suggests we haul ourselves up the cliff. All he asks is that we have a good rest before we attempt the ascent.

The first section up is through tight brush and razor-sharp rattan with small hooks that hold me back like barbed wire. I don't have time to unravel myself, I just yank myself forward. The pain and rips in my skin keep me focused. The cliff starts to become vertical. It is demanding but doable.

We hit the first ledge. Using cracks in the rock, we pull ourselves up. We hit our second ledge. Once again there are enough crevices to gain a purchase. Then we hit the wall—sheer cliff that ends in a green cornice of tangled, moss-covered roots. Momentarily set back, I explore the base of the cliff for a way up. Water drenches us. I drink it in. We could spend the night here in the overhang below the face, but the sight of our goal above us, after working so hard, drives us on.

We have no ropes, no climbing gear, so it will be tough going. Office-building-sized chunks of cliff have fallen off and block our way. Ledges curve up and over our heads. The limestone crumbles off in my hands. Water blinds me and chills me to the bone. I can see why no one has climbed this cliff. Finally I find what I am looking for: a crack in the cliff that will enable me to get tantalizingly close to the green overhang. But more important, a large tree root that will allow us to hike up the clean cliff face above.

I begin to climb, then fall back, a handful of moss and dirt clutched in each hand. Burrowing my hands further in to find something solid, I begin to climb again, slowly and nervously. A slight tug or pressure could bring down tons of rock and trees on top of me.

As I gain in height, the possibility of going back down becomes dimmer and dimmer, making each upward move that much more desperate. My muscles are shaking with exertion as I reach the cornice. My mouth is dry. I am holding onto a snaking tree root that clings to the slippery limestone cliff. What has stopped me is a ledge made of roots, dirt, moss, and plants. A four-foot overhang that doesn't look solid enough to grab onto. For a while I hang there baffled. I cannot get a grip on anything to move myself back and then over. I cannot go down, sideways, or up. My muscles are becoming weak and my energy is leaving me. I lock my legs around the dangling roots and jam my hand into the deep moss. Still nothing to hold onto. But if there is nothing to hold onto, maybe I can use that to my advantage. Desperately I begin to burrow through the roots and moss with my bare hands. Squeezing myself between vines and dirt, I tunnel for my life. Breaking through the dirt and moss, I finally find a tangle of what looks like moss-covered solid rock above me. I wedge my arm in like a stick and throw my leg up to avoid falling back to the rocks below. I am on the ridge.

Covered in dirt my clothes dripping, I weakly yell to Tony that I have made it. I dig through the three-foot-thick carpet of moss searching for a creeper or vine to help Tony up.

Tearing off a creeper, I dangle it down for Tony to tie his pack to. Tony says, "Don't worry. I'll come up with my pack." He begins to climb, using the vine for support. When he reaches the green wall that I had to burrow through, he uses the vine to crawl over. As he tries to lift his leg up for the final push, he pauses, looks at me, and then slowly starts to float downward. I almost laugh as Tony calmly looks at me as he gradually shrinks in size and falls to the rocks below. When he hits, back-first, I don't think he even blinks. No screams, yells, or grunts. He just lies there calmly, eyes wide open. I assume he is dead. I feel detached, a combination of the fuzzy thinking and fatigue.

From down below I hear Tony say quietly, "I think I hurt myself." Surprised he is alive, I ask if he needs assistance.

"No, just let me lie here awhile."

He has fallen a sickening distance. What has saved his life is his fortuitous landing in the crevice of two large moss-covered rocks, moss that is almost three feet thick. Twelve inches either way and he would have had only two inches of moss to cushion the impact.

He rests for quite a while. This time I haul his pack up and then use the vine to bring him all the way up. It is dark now. We shiver with cold as the temperature drops and the sweat from our exertion chills us. It looks like rain.

I find a hollow tree large enough to hold two people in moderate comfort. Lined with fern fronds, it makes a passable bivouac for the night. Tony needs water badly. I find some fetid water in a mosquito-filled hole, but don't tell him where it comes from.

Tony's pack holds a cornucopia of treasures: a tin of sardines, one can of orange juice, newspaper, plastic bags, and a pack of matches.

After planting Tony in his fern bower, I build a fire to dry our clothes and provide some heat. It is not easy to create fire with wood that has been continuously wet, but it works.

I stay awake drying wood and keeping the fire going. When I leave our tiny fern bower, I can't even see or hear the fire from fifteen yards away. A long cold night is made better than passable by the fire and the gnomelike shelter from the rain. I am enjoying myself immensely.

THE WALLS WITHIN

Winnipeg, Manitoba · There were two outdoor activities that were part of the St. John's image. One was canoeing, the other was snowshoeing. In the winter there were long-distance snowshoe trainings that culminated in three levels of marathons. The longest started at the school in Selkirk, ran on the thick ice of the Red River, and ended in Winnipeg to the south. The oldest students would complete a fifty-mile run, the intermediate boys would do twenty-eight, while the youngest were let off easy with an eighteen-mile race. These snowshoe marathons were named after great feats of endurance conducted by French Canadian trappers and explorers like Jean-Baptiste Lagimodière. We would practice every Wednesday after school.

In the winter I also tended to bees I was raising indoors, worked the meat crew, helped on the farm, ran a trapline, got an award in

Roman history, and generally kept busy. On Saturdays we would sell meat door-to-door and on Sundays we would ride the bus into Winnipeg where most boys would see their parents. I would carefully ration my allowance to afford a bus ride to a movie theater where winos could stay out of the cold. There I would watch an endless stream of B movies interrupted by the manager attempting to do a raffle. I would be able to catch the ending of one film, an entire one, and then the beginning of a third before I had to be at church. When the teachers found out what I was doing, they tried to get the other boys' parents to invite me home for dinner, but I preferred the company of winos and the disjointed flow of cheap war movies, jungle flicks, and biker movies to the dysfunctional stolidness of the other boys' homes.

The winter in Selkirk was as cold and brutal as anything you can imagine. Frigid nights, cold air stampeding down from the Arctic, winds howling off the icebound lake north of us, and nothing to stop the wind and snow in the flat prairie. The single-story school buildings were often connected by snow tunnels or trenches because the snow was higher than the rooftops and it was less work to make a tunnel than to clear the snow every day.

As a ten-year-old I was issued a pair of New Brunswick–made moose gut and wood snowshoes. To tie them on, I was also issued four feet of lamp wick, the white flat cotton cord that is used as a wick for kerosene lamps. Snowshoe clothing consisted of soft white moccasins, horsehide gloves with thick woolen liners, a very yellow and very heavy down parka with a wool lining, a long black Voyageurs toque complete with tassel, a wide and very long black wool scarf, and the dubious concept that what we were about to do in the frozen Canadian nights was good for us. I could barely carry all the clothes I was supposed to wear. It took me a good hour to get ready after class on Wednesday as the older boys showed me how to put on long johns, two pairs of heavy jeans, two pairs of wool socks, a heavy shirt, sweat jacket, wool sweater, outer jacket, and then my parka. This was long before arctic clothing had incorporated any lightweight breathable fabric. Older boys also had tricks to keep from freezing. Some put baby oil on their faces, others used their scarves to wrap their parkas more tightly, some had their parents buy them hand warmers and ski gloves. We didn't carry water, wear sunglasses, or even have a first-aid kit. You marched out and you marched back.

I enjoyed the snowshoeing. Walking for hours in blizzards, under starry skies, the constant clacking of our snowshoes mixing with the crunch-crunch-crunching was bearable and gave me time to think. Most problems occurred on the return journey to the school when darkness, windchill, exhaustion, and low morale attacked. Things like blisters, frostbite, snow blindness, or cramps you figured out when you got back.

We snowshoed in teams. There was a leader and followers. I was usually picked as a follower since I was always happy to let the slower members of our team freeze to death rather than listen to their whining and crying. The faster teams had a solution for complaints. When a team member would throw a hissy fit about blisters, missing his mother, or being tired, he was beaten until the idea of moving again seemed like a good idea. We always laughed when the teachers talked about teamwork or how some captains had "whipped their teams into shape."

In the spring the Red River that ran outside the school would begin to break up. One year a military helicopter came to dynamite the ice jams and reduce the flooding. We would watch as our well-worn path across the river and past the church cracked up and floated downriver. Soon it was time to begin canoeing.

Canoeing at St. John's was not of the two-man, summer-camp, fiberglass-hull, tour-the-lake variety. Canoeing meant refurbishing the giant ten-man canvas and wood Chestnut canoes. The idea was to replicate the old voyageur freighter canoes without having to resort to birchbark and pitch. To make sure our historic mission would not be forgotten, the yellow canoes were named after obscure explorers like

David Thompson or slaughtered Jesuit priests like Brébeuf and Marquette. A sign painter would come to paint the black cross and the name on each one.

We didn't just jump in the canoes after they had been spruced up. We had to learn how to dump them, how to carry them, and how to steer them. Then, when school ended for the spring, it was time to load our great yellow canoes on the bus and begin our annual thousand-mile voyage.

ON THE TRAIL OF THE GREAT EXPLORERS

Bagamoyo, Tanzania · Nighttime in the swamps of East Africa. It is raining hard and there is not a lot to see. Surrounded by a solid wall of grass twenty feet high, I sit with three other men in a Land Rover Discovery specially equipped for the Camel Trophy. We are driving very slowly through this almost-impenetrable wall of grass, trying not to fall off the narrow hardened tracks and into the swamps. The powerful driving lights bounce back off the wet grass and illuminate the car like a movie set. I start to realize that what I thought was sweat running down my neck is really dozens of inquisitive insects. Not the big fluttery, elegant kind, but the weird, bizarre bugs of Africa. As we pick up the pace to escape the insects, they get flicked off the wet grass and fall back inside the truck.

Soon we are a furry carpet of prickly grass and crawling insects. It is an indescribable feeling to be soaking wet and covered from head to toe with insects of every variety. Hundreds of cockroaches, beetles, flies, spiders, ticks, moths, crickets, ants, earwigs, and grasshoppers are crawling over and through my hair, up my nose, and inside my clothing. Giant mantises and walking sticks stiffly crawl up my neck to stand next to my head-mounted flashlights and gorge themselves on the gnats, flies, and moths that are attracted to the light. Despite these inquisitive friends, we still have to pay attention to the other surprises that await us in the endless ocean of grass.

Driving through a twelve- to eighteen-foot wall of grass causes stress. It rains every night, swelling rivers, washing out makeshift bridges, and deepening ravines. Fallen tree branches suddenly sprout like lances, straight out of the green wall. In the heavy rain, streambeds present themselves quickly and dramatically and we slam on the brakes to avoid going head over heels into the raging ravines. We get confirmation that we are following what used to be a road when we almost plunge into a ten-foot gap created by two naked bridge supports.

As night turns to day and to night again, all that is around us is grass. At this speed we don't cover much distance. Fording ravines and winching across rivers is our only break from the monotony. There are easier ways to cross the great swamps of Tanzania. Better things to do than try to follow in the footsteps of Burton, Livingston, and Stanley. Much more productive things to do than retrace the great Arab slave route from Bagamoyo to the lake of Ujiji. But that is not why I am here.

The Camel Trophy is an annual event that is part reality, part illusion. Heroic images of stalwart men in yellow Land Rovers battling through tropical hells have earned it the right to apply its own PR slogan: "The Toughest Test of Man and Machine." The idea of the best of the best—hard men in solid trucks pitted against the planet's most hostile regions—has definitely struck a responsive chord in off-roaders and adventurers alike. In truth it began as a bizarre PR concept designed to sell cigarettes. A way to create an event that would project the rugged macho image needed to sell nicotine in countries that banned cigarette advertising. It started when a group of Germans tried to emulate the ad campaign for Camel cigarettes, typically using a photo of a hairy-chested stud and a beat-up jeep in a tropical setting. He was usually lighting a cigarette with a burning stick, rafting his jeep on logs, or doing some type of caveman entertainment. These Germans then decided to drive completely unprepared jeeps across the Amazon. As expected, it was a disaster, but it looked great on film and it fired the imaginations of millions of adventurers.

When R. J. Reynolds took over and pumped in money and publicity, the Camel Trophy exploded. I had read about it in European magazines, and since I loved Land Rovers, jungles, and doing quixotic things, it struck a chord in me. The trouble was the event was not really designed for North America. Canadians or Mexican teams had never existed. They finally let Americans compete because the other countries wanted to beat the U.K. and America to obtain full bragging rights. In 1991 over a million and a half people from seventeen countries vied for the sixty-eight available seats—each one hoping to add to the legend.

A year before, I had called the U.S. team coordinator. He listened patiently and then told me that since I was a Canadian I was out of luck. There were, however, two seats for journalists who worked as a team with the competitors. So I became a journalist. To prove it, I wrote a story of my Borneo expedition for an automotive magazine and sent it to R. J. Reynolds. The lady who handled the PR was suspicious about my enthusiasm and my background in off-roading, Land Rovers, and expeditions, but at the insistence of the team organizer, who knew a ringer when he met one, I was accepted.

Our team consisted of a ponytailed, former army vehicle recovery expert, a tight-lipped motocross racer, and a middle-aged reporter for Voice of America. Three of the most unlikely teammates you could put together. Ideally the team is two men who can only compete once. Many countries like Japan have seasoned hands that show up as journalists each year.

We went through the initial selection trials in the snows of Colorado and then through a faux commando training camp outside Paris. We practiced driving, navigating, winching, rally driving, and coordinating. From the look of it, it would be a disaster. The motocross racer had never competed on a team and in one event grabbed the map and instructions and ran off by himself; the VOA correspondent had the distinction of being the only person to fall off a high-wire bridge; and the vehicle recovery expert kept telling people stories about wars he'd never been in. Me, I just hung out with Coskun, who has been on the Camel Trophy ten times in his career.

After a rousing send-off in Dar es Salaam, where thousands upon thousands of black faces lined the road for miles, we are now in the thick of it.

Ideally the convoy regroups at night, with the teams switching positions daily. This way, by the time the last vehicle gets into camp, the first vehicle's occupants have had a good night's sleep and are ready to leave. But the swamp has thrown everything into disarray.

Instead of building bridges and laying passable tracks for the teams behind, we have been smashing through swamps and washouts, leaving a gooey quagmire for those who follow. The rear of the column has been getting farther and farther behind—first in hours and now days. The vehicles are also starting to suffer from the effects of the difficult terrain. We follow the list of woes over the scratchy radio: a support vehicle has collapsed on a makeshift bridge; the Yugoslavs have rolled their vehicle; the Poles have snapped a winch cable and slingshotted a heavy clevis pin right through a spare wheel, their luggage, and the rear door; the Japanese have bent two steering rods on the exact same rock; and the Germans have rolled their vehicle, burned out their winch, and broken their transfer gear box. In between we can hear the organizer screaming in his thick Scottish accent to keep moving, dammit. Soon we lose radio contact completely.

The tedium of the days and nights is punctuated by dicey rain-swollen-river crossings. During one wet and exhausting crossing I find an unusually large hole through the trees to winch the vehicles up from the river. Once across we collapse until the dawn comes an hour and a half later. The stench of three men who've been sweating in a swamp for two days forces me out onto the roof rack to sleep in the rain. I don't know if I am dreaming or awake when I hear a slow swishing in the grass and wake up to find elephants—big elephants that are quite disturbed to find these yellow intruders blocking their path to the river. Eye-to-eye with these giants, I keep desperately quiet as they slowly squeeze their way alongside our trucks and down to the river.

When the gray dawn arrives, I am soaked to the bone, and through the steamed-up windows my teammates look as if they have been shot dead in their seats: mouths gaping, heads sagging. I realize I wasn't dreaming when I see the huge elephant tracks around the trucks, heading down to the riverbank.

We estimate we are now four days ahead of the main convoy. Our fuel indicators have been on empty for the last day and a half. My eyes have given up focusing—they stare straight ahead. But we are still in good spirits and still find time to marvel at the many unusual sights along the way. When I run over what I first think is a giant toad, it turns out to be the head of a python. It's at least fifteen feet long. Unharmed in the marshy ground, it slithers into the grass.

At last we come to the long-awaited river crossing—the end of wilderness and the beginning of the road that leads to Mikumi. Too tired to walk the swollen river, we charge our vehicle straight ahead, plunging over the edge of a steep rock ledge and submerging our car for the third time that week. Water pours in over the windows as we sit, too tired to care. Finally the motorcycle racer struggles through the heavy current as we pay out the steel winch line. He hooks it up to a tree and signals for us to start winching out of the deep water. As I climb out to help, the Discovery is leaning at a grotesque angle from the pressure of the water. Although the river is now flowing through the open windows of the truck, nothing is happening. The driver is fast asleep at the wheel. I bang on the hood and he finally snaps out of it. We winch it out and our fuel finally runs out twenty feet on the other side. In the last six days we have slept exactly six and one-half hours.

BOREDOM AND DEATH
IN MIKUMI

Mikumi, Tanzania · We have left the mud and grass of the swamps far behind us and are now traveling through classic East African savanna. The rest of the convoy has caught up, although we crashed exactly one-half of the Tanzanian Air Force to do it—the Huey I loaded up with spare parts and fuel never made it back. But that and the mud and the rain are a distant dream.

Now I am in the Africa of my dreams. The horizon offers a virtually unobstructed 360-degree view. Puffy, white clouds form an endless pattern interrupted only by gentle acacias and tortured, swollen baobab trees. Gracefully bobbing giraffes watch shyly in the distance. Time slows down and my senses are sharpened. I begin to notice the thousands of purple and yellow flowers that carpet the land. Time passes even more slowly as vultures aimlessly circle the convoy. We discover bleached, tuskless skeletons of elephants killed by poachers. I suck up the heat and smells of the savanna.

My once-soaked clothes and body are now dry. My hands have become hard, cracked, and callused, the nails and creases packed with black dirt. The hot sun has begun to tan my skin and clear up the rashes, grass cuts, and insect bites. I am adapting to the hot, dry savanna days and cool, crisp nights. I come to recognize the unique flora and fauna of the spear grass. Thousands of these sharp, barbed weapons are snicked off by the brush guard and become embedded in skin and clothing. However, spear grass pales in comparison to the various types of acacia thorns that grow up to five inches long. Like porcupine quills, these light, hollow daggers penetrate right through heavy boots and soft flesh.

I become good friends with the scourge of Africa—the tsetse fly.

Anatomically like deerflies, but with mandibles designed to bite through water buffalo skin, they constantly attack me. The unlucky ones explode in a shower of blood. Cattle cannot live where there are tsetse flies, so only wild animals and poachers roam here. Elephants, warthogs, baboons, giraffes, zebras, gazelles, and other savanna animals do not have the bored indifference of game parks. They are untrusting, nervous, and keep their distance. In the Selous, a game preserve in Tanzania, a family of elephants plays in the shade of a spreading acacia tree. The bull elephant suddenly takes exception to our intrusion and turns on us, ears flapping, shaking his head and loudly trumpeting his displeasure. A false charge. Confident we are leaving, he stops short and saunters off.

Soon the soil turns from black loam to dark red clay; the weather turns softer, more tropical; and for some reason the people become gentler and shier. It is also darker and more foreboding. The wild, empty panoramas of Tanzania are replaced by the heavily populated, patchwork agricultural quiltwork of Burundi. Slipping and sliding through muddy banana plantations, the convoy labors over a mountain pass in dense fog. As we reach the crest, we are dazzled by the brilliant light and spectacular view.

Before us lies a wide expanse of shimmering silver, fronting a mountainous wall of dark green. A massive wall of mountains stretches as far as the eye can see. Above these magnificent mountains are huge, white thunderheads and below is the fabled Sea of Ujiji, now known as Lake Tanganyika.

We have endured the swamps, the long, hot savanna, the wild animals, the pests, and pestilence. It is time to celebrate. That evening's festivities at the Source du Nil hotel in Bujumbura include a performance by native drummers, a speech by the president of Burundi, and polite conversations with the cream of Burundian society. We are quite a novelty here; most people don't quite know what to make of us.

We finish sixth, the victims of unbounded energy and circumstance. Coskun and the Turks are the winner.

We wait patiently for the officials to present their awards and make their speeches. Then it is time for the real celebration. One by one the team members start throwing each other into the pool. The highlight of the event is an organizer pulling a knife on me when I try to throw him in the pool wearing his kilt. He shows up later in his normal outfit but is ignored by the rowdy participants. Soon there are more people in the pool than outside. After we run out of khaki-clad people, everything else goes in: Sabena stewardesses, lawn furniture, waiters, pots and pans. Laughing riotously, we pour what beer is left on top of each other's heads and swap our team shirts with new friends. Soon Americans become Russians, Turks become Italians, Greeks become British—until the whole room is a true United Nations of soaking-wet, half-drunk adventurers. It takes a few hours to empty the hotel's beer supply, then we head out into the streets looking for an all-night spot. Dripping wet, singing and laughing, we stagger through the dangerous streets of Bujumbura until boredom and sleep set in.

EN ROULANT

Rocky Mountain House, Alberta · We made the long drive to Rocky Mountain House in the yellow school bus. On top of the overloaded GMC sat our yellow canvas freighter canoes and inside were piled green duffel bags and rations. Hardtack, peanut butter, porridge, and Spam. Although we had spent the last few months paddling in front of the school, I had not yet learned how to set up for big rapids, how to pick my spot carefully and then pull like hell to survive, how to measure depth by reading the ripples and light on the water, how to listen to what the river is telling me.

I learned a lot as we paddled and carried the ponderous four-hundred-pound canoes. They were built to take a brutal pounding on rocks and rivers, although their yellow paint slowly wore off as we drove them down the Saskatchewan. I wore canvas shoes, a yellow mackinaw hat for the sun, jeans, and a T-shirt. My days on the river were pretty mundane. Up at daybreak, a breakfast of burned porridge, fried Spam, and moldy hardtack. Then roll up the wet canvas tents, our wet bags, clean our aluminum mess tins with river sand, stiffly get in the canoe and start another long northern day of paddling. I didn't steer. That was left to an adult. I just paddled.

When we got tired, our steersman would scream at us and usually whack the slowest one with his paddle blade. The more experienced steersman were cool, but if you pulled a neophyte volunteer he invariably exploded in sputtering rages and would vent his frustrations on any "lily dippers," our term for kids that made it look like they were paddling but wouldn't pull hard.

In the beginning the rapids were numerous and it wasn't unusual for a canoe to dump its contents into the foaming, icy water and then be carried to a backwater as the spluttering crew fetched their bobbing duffel bags and camp gear. I remember large, sixty-foot whirlpools that would open up and close like something from a horror film. Most rapids went by in a blur—you just paddled for your life. It was then I learned from the others' mistakes: how to use the current instead of fighting it, when to enter the cyclical thundering of ridged waves that would rise and fall.

Days were too long in the high northern latitudes. We would eat our dinner in an exhausted haze and drop off to sleep. In the early spring temperatures would drop and sometimes I would awake in a puddle covered with ice. The inside of my wet sleeping bag would be warm and womblike, but my socks were frozen so stiff I had to put them under my armpits to straighten them out. Those that did not heed the early morning wake-up call were dealt with harshly.

I soon learned the trick of sleeping in the frigid night without a sleeping bag, exhaustion quickly rendering me unconscious, and being awakened at dawn by the sound of my teeth chattering. I was in my element. By draining every ounce of my ability I could become transcendent, be perfectly content in the gray light of dawn while others slept. Sometimes I would watch the other children in their ugly sleep, lying dirty and motionless. With their mouths parted, eyes open, and teeth showing, they looked like cadavers awaiting burial. I was no longer of that world.

THE ROLL OF A HEAD

Srinagar, Kashmir · The plane slams down, rocking me forward against my seat belt. I should be looking at the mountain scenery but all I notice are rows of bunkers on each side of the runway as we whiz past, silver MiG-21s and large camouflage transport planes ready to take off. They come in fast here because the mujahideen have Stinger antiaircraft missiles. As I disembark, there are twenty soldiers ringing our plane, guns at the ready. I am here to look for ghosts.

The story is confusing. Some say they found the blond-haired, suntanned head of Hans Christian Ostro balanced between his legs for effect, others say the head was found forty meters away. Some say that the words "Al-Faran" were carved with a knife on his back; others say they were carved on his chest. All agree that the Norwegian tourist was beheaded while still alive. This is not what Kashmir claims happens to its tourists, not to Westerners who are simply visiting what has been called among the most beautiful and historic parts of Asia. But it happened.

News of the trouble piled up quickly at first: an American escaped, a Norwegian was killed, others were sick, rescue attempts failed . . . or were there rescue attempts? There were conflicting reports of shoot-outs, executions, sightings, and supposed burials. And then silence. The families searched desperately but in vain. The world's best intelligence groups searched in vain. Over half a million Indian troops searched in vain. Then, as dramatically as the story appeared, it disappeared. Not surprising since the Westerners were about 1 percent of the 548 people kidnapped in Kashmir in that same year. More than 2,000 people have been kidnapped in Kashmir in the last decade, and fewer than half of them have survived, statistics that are lost among the 25,000 people killed—about fifty deaths a week. Something evil is happening in northwestern India. I go.

My fellow travelers, who I thought were businessmen or returning locals, turn out to be journalists here to cover the swearing in of a new government. My plan is to stay at Adhoo's, a well-known hotel for journalists, and then head into the countryside. My cabdriver has other ideas. He extols the beauty of houseboats, the joys of trekking, and the ecstasy that awaits me in the trout streams high up in the mountains. Because he has a polite and unnerving habit of looking directly at me from the front seat when he drives, I say that's nice, but for now please shut up, turn around, and drive.

The convoluted and crowed road into town is overseen by a massive military presence. My newfound guide advises me sotto voce when to not take pictures, saying "military" as we approach each sandbagged bunker. I make him very nervous by taking pictures of the checkpoints as well as the scenic spots. The blast marks and nervous state of patrolling soldiers indicate that when my guide speaks of the various attacks that have occurred here, it is not a history lesson but something immediate and real.

The journalists have beaten me to the hotel. Much to my chagrin, there are no vacant rooms. All the other hotels in town are occupied by the military. What to do? Well, the houseboat doesn't sound too bad now. My driver seems quite pleased, since he happens to have a cousin who owns a houseboat.

The British began the custom of residing in houseboats because they could not own land. The ornately carved boats became de rigueur in the seventies for marijuana-smoking tourists who could indulge themselves in the local weed, safe from the police on land.

Dal Lake is lined by 980 houseboats with romantic-sounding names that now sit empty. The long, gently curved rectangular barge has a porch at the entrance and bedrooms toward the back. There is also a large sitting room, dining room, and extra bedrooms.

The owner of a particularly fine houseboat next door to the one I choose to stay at tells me it took eight people working for five years to create his twenty-by-eighty-foot masterpiece. Curving gently upward at each end, it is built of fragrant deodar, a local cedar that comes from the mountains. As I talk to my neighbor, it becomes evident that the investment of so much money during a time where there are no tourists was not the wisest thing. But he was never in it to make any money, just pride in the beautiful craftsmanship. Someday, when the tourists return, he will have enough money to furnish it. As I get in a *shikara*, or small canoe, to visit his house, my host, who is returning from the opposite shore, assumes that I am jumping ship for his neighbor's boat and screams, "Wait, wait, I am coming, I am coming!"

It's not too profitable to lose track of your tourists around here.

I decide to go for a walk in the old town as the sun sets over the deep blue mountains. The owner of my houseboat, nervous about my visiting his neighbor, offers to come along, or rather insists.

I like the cool, crisp, colonial atmosphere of Srinagar. The solidly built, British-style mansions that overlook the lake give the city the feel of being an upscale resort, which of course it once was. These homes are now occupied by Kashmiris who sell carpets, rice, and wool.

Along the narrow streets are shops where carvers, weavers, and other craftspeople create the intricate handicrafts and goods the area is known for. The Kashmiris are excellent craftspeople and the long winters and lack of professional jobs give them plenty of time to create meticulously ornate carpets, papier-mâché, and needlework. Most of them work by the golden glow of a single, flyspecked lightbulb. Almost all the families in the towns work the looms or carve during the winter to earn money. Their goods are usually sold by local co-ops, which once provided an important supplement to the summer tourism income. Now there is no summer tourism income and India does not allow wholesale exportation of these goods. Therefore, tourists must come to India to buy these goods. The problem is there are no tourists anymore.

There is little evidence of tension here as the sun sets. True, the walls and streets are decorated with green scrawls of graffiti—JK-LF for Jammu Kashmir Liberation Front or AZ-JK for Harkut Jammu Kashmir. But children play, women cook, and men smoke as if it is just another day. When I mention to my guide, Ahmad, that I have seen this graffiti in Pakistan, he is surprised that I know what this means. I explain to him that a few months ago I was on the other side of the border where the Harkut and other groups are very visible in big offices complete with neon signs. When I say the word "liberation" for the second time, he uncharacteristically says, "That is all bullshit."

I ask him what he means.

"They do not want liberation, they are just using us," he answers.

Ahmad, who is Muslim, asks me if I like Muslims. I say yes. He asks me what I think of the Taliban, whom I visited a few months earlier in Afghanistan. He asks in the same manner someone would ask you about a football team. He is uncomfortable with the image Muslims have in this Hindu-dominated region. It is portrayed as Muslim mujahideen against Hindu soldiers, but in reality it is the ordinary Kashmiris who are dying.

Walking back to the houseboat in the dark, I find myself in the middle of a night patrol; twelve men are spaced twenty meters apart (in case of grenade or mine attack), carrying submachine guns at the ready. There is no curfew tonight, but anyone out on the streets after 8:30 better have a good reason. The night is when the mujahideen attack and the soldiers make it clear from the looks they give me that they don't like my presence.

The next morning Ahmad greets me by saying, "Please hurry, our cabdriver is afraid." Hyperventilating would be a better term. Only five people were killed yesterday, but today is a special day. The new government will be sworn in and the mujahideen have called for a general strike. This means shops must be closed, no one is to work, and truck drivers and cabdrivers are to stay home. Along the road there are soldiers every twenty to fifty feet. There is no civilian traffic allowed, only armored military vehicles. Naturally this is the day I have chosen to take a drive in the country.

As we drive out of the city and toward the mountains, Ahmad points to certain spots and intersections. All that can be seen are bunkers with blast marks from previous attacks. Pointing out recent grenade attacks instead of scenic wonders seems to be the standard patter of guides and cabdrivers.

We pass through yellow rice fields on roads bordered by poplars and sycamores turning gold in the autumn weather. The blue snow-covered mountains in the distance are clean and pure against the trees and fields. The only reminder that we are in a hot zone is the constant presence of passing armored troop carriers, road patrols, and various checkpoints.

The scenery of the countryside is spectacular, so I have to get some photos. I get out and walk through the rice paddies, now dry and mature. Men and women from the villages squat on their haunches and, using a small sickle, snick off handfuls of rice stalks that are left to dry in the sun. Later the stalks will be threshed over a rock or wooden bench. The warm sun on my back, the crunch of the sickles, and the beehive-shaped mounds of rice stalks make for a very bucolic setting.

Wrapped up in photographing this rural scene, I unknowingly step right into a concealed machine-gun nest and almost trip over the barrel of a 50-caliber gun. The two camouflaged soldiers are polite, but urgently direct me away from their post.

Getting back into the car, I begin to wonder just how much I think I see and how much I don't see.

We continue our trip to the front lines, our taxi clattering up the mountain toward the border. As we sign in at the military checkpoint guarded by Gurkhas, I notice in the logbook that two Taiwanese tourists passed through here the day before. A few miles later the road disappears. It has been taken away by a landslide. There are horsemen, or pony wallahs, waiting here. The horses formerly carried tourists around the hills, but the horsemen say they have been sitting where the road is washed out for ten days without seeing tourists. The Taiwanese never made it this far, so they must have turned back at the checkpoint or given up when they saw the road was washed out.

Gulmarg is the site of an eighteen-hole golf course (the world's highest) and a rather impressive ski lift built by a Swiss company and surrounded by rustic chalets. Now the hotels are empty and falling apart, the ski lift is in pieces. The golf course is kept well cropped by grazing goats and today there is one family sitting peacefully on an abandoned putting green enjoying the scenery.

I hire small mountain ponies to take us up to the vale of Khilanmarg and then the mountain of Apharwat.

My anemic horse, Peter, keeps tripping over my legs, which I have to hold up to keep from dragging on the ground. My pony wallah says that Peter is small because he had little to eat when growing up. I offer to switch and carry Peter up the mountain and the horseman laughs.

As we ride through Gulmarg and up into the mountains, I ask Ahmad if there are mujahideen here. He says occasionally the guides see groups of twenty to forty armed men in the forest, but it is best to turn in the opposite direction. Has anybody seen the hostages here? No, but there is a rumor that they were spotted walking toward Jammu in the Kishtawar area. Kishtawar is beyond the southeasternmost point of Kashmir and we are on its northwesternmost point. There have been many sightings and rumors of sightings of the hostages, but this one makes sense, as it is impossible to survive high in the mountains. Even the shepherds go down in the winter.

If I thought I could come here and learn all there is to know about the hostage situation without any probing, I would have been very disappointed. And, as I expected, the locals are hesitant to discuss anything; and the military has no idea where they are, although they say they know.

I want to see how close we can get to the border. The horses cannot walk in the steep, deep snow, so we climb until the snowdrifts become too high. It is cold now and I am not dressed for alpine exploration. A military camp looms on the summit above. My guide says going farther is ill advised. "From this point two things will happen. Either we will be shot at by the military or we will freeze to death." Realizing that the Pakistani military is not looking for overnight patrons and that we have four to five hours to return, I turn back.

As we descend we chat with some shepherds who are laying in winter feed for their animals. A small calf bleats. The shepherd says it has been born too late and will not make it through the winter. They will kill it and head down in a week or so. Have they seen anything? The old shepherd's tan and weathered face tells me he has not lived this long by chatting about such things to strangers. He just smiles and poses for pictures with his daughter.

In truth I didn't come here to find the hostages—it would take great conceit to assume that I can learn something that the relatives, FBI, CIA, SAS, GS-9, and other intelligence and military special operations groups have not—but rather to understand the lay of the land and background of the conflict in Kashmir. The abducted Westerners are not the first hostages to be taken here and they will not be the last. Sometimes knowledge requires studying the obvious and the circumstantial. More important, I am trying to understand how every traveler's nightmare occurred in the hope that others will not have to enter the same dark underworld.

THE WAY OF
THE WILDERNESS

Selkirk, Manitoba · When I arrived at the eighteenth-century stone former priory house just north of Selkirk on the Red River in what was the second month of my tenth year, all I had been told was that I would be going away to school. Like a soldier being sent off to basic training, I assumed that it couldn't be all that bad, just different than what I was used to.

Life at St. John's was different. Nothing compared to the internal brutality of the first week. The concept of angry, often troubled children thrown in with bright, religious, or other students by well-meaning or negligent parents is something that makes *Lord of the Flies* pale in comparison. No one wanted to be there, and many of the kids had been thrust into the school by parents with the same misconceptions I had: that it was a nice school where you got to do a lot of outdoor things—like stay alive. The fighting started on the first evening as sobbing children were pounded by second-year veterans who stole their possessions, picked a fight, and just generally funneled their aggression toward the innocent newcomers. It didn't take me long to figure out that each student must fight for his position in the hierarchy. Wimp out and you became the butt of jokes. Fight back and the big kids picked on the next wimpiest kid. Look for comfort or rescue from the teachers and the beatings and ridicule became even more intense.

From my lonely perspective as the youngest boy it seemed that the older you got, or the more years you spent at the school, the easier it was. To me the casual ambience of the grade-twelve room seemed country-clubbish and relaxed. But where I lived, towel fights, silent beatings, french sheeting, pudding powder in beds, acid on toilet seats, and other cruel tricks were part of my new life.

In addition there was the punishment meted out to us by the teachers. In a brutal backlash to what the staff considered permissive times corporal punishment was a fact of life on a regular basis. The paddle was the weapon of choice. Each teacher had his own personal opinion and style of punishment. Some preferred narrow hardwood for speed and impact; others went wider and softer to minimize tissue damage. Some just grabbed anything at hand. The usual punishment was between five and twenty very painful blows on the posterior, usually leading to bruising and numbness.

I did my share of bending over and staring at my shoes while a teacher whaled away on me. I can't say that it ever did anything other than make me be more careful the next time I broke a rule.

THE PROPHET

Srinagar, Kashmir · Unsuccessful in my attempt to learn about the hostages, I am back at my houseboat. There I talk to an eighty-year-old who was a travel guide in the forties. While puffing away on his "hubbly bubbly," as the British used to call hookahs, he reflects on the state of his country. Speaking in an archaic form of colonial British, he talks of how his country used to be "damned cheap" and how he was "a jolly chap" in his youth. He recounts the joy of tourists when he showed them his country and tells me how much he loves fly-fishing, hiking, and camping. But with the war, not to mention his bad legs and old age, all that is over. Nevertheless it is still his country. This is a statement that the mujahideen and Indian Army cannot make yet.

Changing the subject, I ask him about the tomb of Yusaf and his eyes light up.

"You know about this?" he asks excitedly.

I tell him what I have read and heard: that Jesus wandered as far as India between the ages of twelve and twenty-five and returned to his beloved Kashmir after his "staged" crucifixion. Some Kashmiris believe that their valley is the true promised land and some believe that they are descended from one of the lost tribes of Israel. According to local legend, Jesus was known as St. Yuz Asaf, a man who performed miracles and preached in the first century A.D. Jesus' Hebrew name is Yazu.

I ask him what he knows about the tomb. He says the tomb contains the body of Yusaf. I ask him when Yusaf was buried there.

"Four thousand years ago, before there was history," the old man says.

So much for accurate historical recall.

Who is Yusaf?

"He is your prophet and he is our prophet. Yusaf is all around us," he says. "He is everywhere, everything. When you breathe in and out, that is Yusaf. Everything around you is Yusaf."

Not knowing quite where to go with this outburst of religious enthusiasm, I ask if the man in the tomb is Jesus Christ. He says quite frankly that he doesn't know.

As I go to bed my guide says, "Make sure you make yourself very clean tomorrow." He even tells me how to wipe the dust off my hiking boots. "We must be very clean for Yusaf."

The next day we head for the tomb of Yusaf. It is in a nondescript building near the famous wooden mosque of Srinagar. The mosque was originally built in 1385 and has been burned and rebuilt five times since. Constructed with wood shingles and three hundred cedar trunks, the mosque retains its medieval look and also seems to retain its inflammatory character. It is the flash point for most demonstrations and resultant violence in Srinagar.

All traffic is prohibited from entering this area, but we cajole the police into letting us pass. Large blue APCs with turret gunners roar up and down the street around the mosque. People gather to make their prayers at the mosque. My guide prays and kisses the ornaments as we enter.

Inside is a glass container and within that a faded, dusty, shroud-covered tomb. A cement block inset with a pair of unauthentic-looking footprints sits nearby. Otherwise there is nothing. Is this the tomb of Christ? Does it matter? Is there a reason why he has chosen this beautiful but troubled land? Why would a prophet be in a Muslim country run by Hindus surrounded by Buddhists?

Outside the dirty windows, I can see the seeds of riot between the Kashmiri Muslims and Hindu soldiers. I wonder if whoever is buried here can hear my guide's Muslim prayers for peace. Like the hostages, this is an enigma whose need for a solution is overshadowed by the harsh reality of survival. But my trip to this tomb taught me that it is important to understand that the Kashmiris can accept these enigmas without facts or resolution. I think I have found my answer. The hostages are here and they are not here. Kashmir is a war zone and it is a tourist haven. It is whatever it must be for people to survive.

THE SILENCE

Somewhere on the North Saskatchewan River · After my first year I never really was the same. I had lost my quick laugh, my ready smile. I stood silently, awkward and uncomfortable around adults. By then I had paddled every inch of one thousand miles, my nose and ears cracked and bleeding, my face dark from the sun, my eyes bleached from staring into the sparkling water. I looked like I had survived something terrible. I was only ten years old and I had the eyes of Jesus on the cross.

I had also learned how to twist sausages and butcher meat. My inexperience with a butcher knife and general clumsiness made deep cuts in my hands. Salting hams in ice-cold brine was a memorable experience. There was also the unique unofficial punishment accorded the meat crew by other students. We had two incinerator-like smokers that stood black and tall. Hams were hung inside and wood chips placed in a pan below. After these were ignited I would be thrust in with the greasy, salty hams and the choking smoke, the other students would slam the heavy steel door shut and turn the flames up beneath my dancing feet. My muffled screams and shaken appearance when I emerged, clothes smoking and smoldering sneaker soles, always evoked hilarious laughter.

One of my escapes was to snowshoe out into the woods surrounding the school. Stealing some bacon I had just sliced and packaged, I would put on my yellow parka, walk out into the silent, perfect snow, find an isolated spot, and cook it over a crackling fire of birch wood.

My favorite times were when it snowed. I would sit and be caressed by the heavy snowflakes as they danced around me. The snow-laden trees and winter silence would soothe me. Only then could I escape the hard reality of where I was and just enjoy the moment. I discovered there was something pure, inarguably elegant and right in places you never expected, a place and time that would let you see further than your everyday existence. I was alone, perfect, focused in a soft, whitened land.

THE SHADOW

Somewhere over Texas · Sitting on a plane flying to a television conference in New Orleans to plug my TV show, I am seated next to a man who looks like a younger Marlon Brando, hawk-nosed with clear skin, china-blue eyes, and silvering hair. He is wearing a large, very used, very faded green army coat. There is a green "Budweiser"—the SEAL camouflage patch—and SEAL Team One patch crudely sewn on his left shoulder. His shirt is worn and frayed, his sunglasses cheap and scratched. He could be a plumber, truck driver, or another SEAL wannabe. He notices I am reading a history of the SEALs and he asks to look, then thumbs through looking for a specific year.

He points out people he knows. He points out mistakes "Hell, he didn't die in the crash, that rocket went right through him. I know. I was there." He flips to the chapter on Grenada, the debacle where a number of SEALs were dropped off too far from shore and never seen again: "Tadpoles, I trained."

He hands the book back with a look of disgust. There is something locked inside him. But then he spoke quietly.

"I should write a book but someone from the NSA will tap me on the shoulder and take me away. We 'did' fifty for every one SEAL we lost, the ones they kept track of." He is staring intently into my eyes, looking for a signal that it is worth telling these stories. We have plenty of time and there is no one around us. We are locked in a sharp pool of light from the overhead reading light.

SEAL Team One was an integral part of Phoenix, an organized assassination and intelligence-gathering program that decimated much of the Viet Cong infrastructure in two rounds, beginning in 1966 and 1968. Officially the SEALs only engaged in gathering information, but SEAL Team One records are still classified. You don't train and use SEALs just to gather documents. Their exploits in Vietnam revolve around the heroic, the crazy, and the secret. They made the Viet Cong cadre and tax collectors disappear. He tells the stories as if he has found someone he can deposit them with.

"The train was twenty-five klicks inside China and there was a U-2 that just happened to be overhead when it blew up. I can't say who did it but, boy, were they pissed.

"I told the brass that Hamburger Hill was hollow, an arms cache, but CBS Television was there, so Westmoreland wanted a body count. We told 'em one five-hundred bomb would blow the whole place up.

"Yeah I should write a book someday but it would have to be fiction."

There is a natural pause in our conversation. I wonder why his skin is so light and uncreased after the twenty-four years he said he had been in Asia. Then I realize expats are like that. They stay out of the sun.

He resumes as if there was no pause.

"You ever seen one of those things you turn upside down and it snows?" He jiggles his hand to indicate a snow dome. "It was like that in the Huey.

"The Viet Cong were in the trees and we had come into the LZ the wrong way. The bullets would punch through the walls of the helicopter and blow out chunks of the insulation. It was crazy in there. The pilot was trying to disconnect the rotor or something and we crashed pretty hard."

I realize he is describing a story I just read in the book on SEALs, but he is setting the record straight. He was there. The truth is important. It's what he fought for.

"My claim to fame was pulling my .45 on the pilot to make him take off. But he wouldn't. I also went a little crazy and threatened a doctor to force him to operate. I was an E5 then but I went out as an E3."

There is a long pause. This one not as natural as the first.

"Hey, I got the job done."

Another pause while he takes the book back again.

"You ever heard of the Fabian Society?"

"No."

"You don't know who General Fabius Maximus is? That's the first thing they teach you in Military College."

Pulling back, he looks at me more closely. He has been deceived by my knowledge of the jargon, the places, the names. He realizes he has made a mistake. I am not an operator, have never been a meat-eater or even a tadpole. I may have the look, the walk, and the talk but I am not one of his own.

Cautioned, he shifts to stories that have more distance. Discussing Diem and his need for a Catholic state, it's as if he is quoting from an intel report nobody in the State Department bothered to read. He is almost apologetic.

"Somebody took the umbrella of security away from him. He got hit by a big chunk. One month later Kennedy was assassinated—coincidence?"

I don't know. Maybe he doesn't know. Or maybe he does.

I mention how things have changed in the SEALs. He says, "Yeah, they got rid of all the dinosaurs." I mention the Mormons but he doesn't take the bait, dismissing it by saying, "They recruit certain places. God-fearing people. Certain ethnic types. Always has been that way, even on the civilian side."

He is alluding to the tight linkage between special forces and the CIA.

He continues: "SEALs were men out of their time. When they came home in the seventies, they were baby killers, assassins . . . The Budweiser was a black mark for everyone but a SEAL."

There is a pause.

"But we got the job done."

I have never thought of what I do as a duty. I have never even considered writing fiction to communicate fact. I had signed up, charged into the fray with both guns blazing, and hoped that at the end of tour I wouldn't realize I had made the wrong choice. My new friend was so deeply hidden in the shadows it caused me pain. What if you got the job done and nobody cared? What if you knew the truth and nobody listened?

What if your soul was on fire, the inside of your head was full of snow, and nobody came to save you?

PARADISE FOUND

Victoria, British Columbia · They say children never truly absorb horror but then again they never forget it either. It sits patiently on a bench outside their psyche waiting for a crack in the door. In our infrequent correspondence I had no interest in telling my mother the things that went on at St. John's. And she, mistaking my silence and reserve as maturity, declared herself happy that I was "becoming a man."

My mother had moved to Victoria and begun sending me the tourist brochures from this quaint seaside bastion of heavy Tudor homes, moss-covered oak trees, and massive stone government buildings. Here in this quaint corner of "ye olde" whatever were hanging flower baskets, grown men dressed up as Beefeaters, flowers on the streetlamps, tacky wax museums, gaudy gardens, colorful totem poles, horse-drawn carriages, haunted cottages, and grand stone buildings. I read and reread the brochures throughout the year, wondering if this was to be my reward for enduring my schooling.

So when the end of the school year came and our canoe trip was over, I couldn't wait to go to Victoria.

The only problem with my entry to paradise was that, from what I was told, the school never received my mother's new address or phone number. As one by one the students were picked up until finally I was the only one left, the teachers politely asked me what I was going to do that summer. I didn't really know.

The school contacted an Anglican minister who lived in Victoria who would pick me up at the airport and help me find my mother. The minister drove a Volvo and lived in a spectacular home complete with Haida carvings and paintings. His friends and the people we met remarked on my quiet demeanor, my lanky frame, and the pale gray of my eyes—eyes that cut through people like a razor.

Every day we would drive along the ocean to see if I could recognize a house or apartment. I didn't have the heart to tell him that my mother had never told me a thing. After a few days he declared success.

My mother didn't seem to be too worried about the minister's concern. She thanked him like he was delivering groceries and he left perplexed. I could tell that even though my mother was happy to see me she was also shocked. I was undernourished, quiet, severely sunburned, and coldly alone. Like most children, I did what I was told, didn't focus on the big picture or even try to make sense out of what I was doing. But being near the ocean gave me a purpose; we lived in a tiny rented cabin above the beach. I immediately began to explore every inch of the rugged, rocky coastline and spend every day near the water, making rafts and setting sail into the open ocean, only returning when they fell apart and I was forced to swim. I would spend enormous amounts of time picking out penny candy at the corner store, climbing the rocky hills, examining sea life, and enjoying Victoria. Once in a while my brother and I would visit one of the attractions that I had carefully memorized from the tourist brochures. I loved the cartoons of Norris, who depicted stuffy old English pensioners, little old ladies, and other Victorian clichés.

But despite my mother's enthusiasm for her return to the city of her childhood and my happiness in being here, it seemed that I needed more time to get the full benefit of St. John's. Betrayed again. I didn't cry, I had nothing to say. The stewardess on the plane saw me flying alone and gave me a plastic airplane and coloring book. I thanked her politely. I was twelve years old but I was not a child. I would rather just look out the window quietly.

OVER THE LINE

Phnom Penh, Cambodia · That night, back in Siem Reap, we go to a nightclub. The sign outside says "no guns or explosives." The music is pure singsong Khmer played at ear-damaging levels. The Khmers respond to the music in a circular line dance reminiscent of a bad country line dance. My friend Wink decides to get up and jam with the band. The audience is dumbstruck and stares openmouthed for two songs, not knowing if they should clap or cover their ears. After Wink sits down, it seems not everyone is thrilled with his impromptu jam session. We are challenged to a fight in a less-than-sensitive manner: an elbow not once, not twice, but three times in the back—hard. We decide to split. This would not be a John Wayne punch-'em-up, but probably a good ol' sloppy burst of gunfire. As we change venues, a group of surly Cambodian men follows us out into the street. We face off, neither side wanting to be the first to start hostilities. Luckily at this point our driver pulls up and we drive off.

We stop at another place with the same bad music, same knife-edge tension. Wink sums it up by saying, "These people are very fucked up." The more genteel would say they suffer from post-traumatic stress, though Cambodians aren't even aware of the term, they just deal with it in that polite, quiet way. There has been too much killing here. There is still a lot of rage and sadness. A Malaysian friend expressed a similar sentiment to me on hearing that I would be going to Cambodia: "The people there are very quiet and very angry—they have seen too much." The Vietnamese invaded, then the United Nations invaded. Now Cambodia is getting to its feet unsteadily. At the moment we are surrounded by the legacy of the U.N. peacekeepers: prostitutes and nightclubs.

We sit with three Cambodian girls; or, rather, three girls make a hurried grab for the empty chairs at our table. Westerners are big game for bar girls. Wink chats with them in Vietnamese. In Cambodia most working girls are divided into "go dancing girls," women who sit, talk, and dance with and maybe sleep with you on request, and "taxi girls," who are simply for sex. There are also houses where the function of intercourse is emotionally and financially comparable to the drive-through window at McDonald's. Most of the girls are Vietnamese, but the girls at our table are Cambodian. To prove it, they mimic the ancient hand movements and music of the *apsara*, the temptresses seen on the temples at Angkor. Wink is surprised, since most girls who were trained dancers were killed by the Khmer Rouge. Aspiring to more intellectual entertainment, we teach one of the girls a few English words at her request. She tells us that if she learns English, she will get a better job. We find out that what she means is that she can sleep with more Westerners and therefore make more money. She tells us with some pride that one Japanese man actually paid her forty dollars for the whole night.

Sitting outside to avoid the chilling air-conditioning and deafening noise inside, we are interrupted by a Cambodian cop flying out of the glass entry doors, followed by shouting, punching, and kicking patrons. The girls sitting with us immediately jump up, then drag us around the corner and down an alley. They plead with us to "Go, go, run! Please, before you are shot!" Not quite knowing what they are talking about, we try to walk back to the front to watch the fight, but the girls push us back, pleading with us to run away.

We push past them and are in time to watch the cop being kicked, beaten, and then slammed unconscious before being thrown into the back of a pickup truck. The girls explain that we are lucky (a term we are hearing a lot here), that usually there is gunfire. They mimic the action of someone firing a machine gun. One tells us that this week "a man fell down, went to sleep." I laugh. The expression on the girl's face tells me that she is not trying to be cute; she is trying to avoid saying the word "died." She halfheartedly repeats the machine-gun pantomime and tries to make me understand. The sad look in her eyes tells me that I am being far too casual about a very real threat. With a sense of resignation she says, "This is a dangerous place. You should not be here."

PARADISE LOST

Selkirk, Manitoba · In my first year at St. John's my teacher set up a science experiment with rats. They lived in a three-by-four glass cage and were fed and maintained as part of a science project while the boys were in school. When the kids left for the summer, no one remembered to do anything with the rats. When I returned for the new year, I came across the rat cage. It was easy to find because of the smell. The rats were living in a bed of rotting and consumed rat corpses, packed tight with feces; despite this they had been able to breed and eat enough of their own young to survive. I felt an odd kinship with those rats, since they were originally brought in by a teacher to help the new boys deal with their homesickness and loneliness.

By now school was routine. I enjoyed shoveling the mountains of chicken manure, staying up all night with new piglets, watching mosquito eggs hatch, and trying to trap enough small, furry animals on my trapline to make a pair of mitts. When the other boys would discuss what they did on their breaks or what they did at home, I kept silent.

When Christmas break came, the staff looked around for someone to take my brother and me in. I spent Christmas at the home of a fellow classmate. His parents were farmers and I enjoyed myself. I even started oil painting. For the first time I was in a normal family and it didn't seem that hard. When the next holiday came, I spent it with another family. Then one day I received a letter from my mother. It was a nice letter, but it said that I would be living with my father from now on. I read and reread the letter to see if I was understanding it right. I smelled the paper and looked at the indentations for some clue that it could be a joke or a forgery. Then I threw it away, cried tears of embarrassment. I had been inventing reasons why I couldn't go home and now my mother had repaid my odd sense of loyalty by abandoning me. Some time later my father drove up to the school and confirmed that my brother and I would be living with him. In his clumsy way he apologized for letting this happen. He had seen me only once after my first year at St. John's. Once he looked around at the school he left with tears in his eyes.

COLD GOING OVER

Pendjikent, Tajikistan · Hamrakul says, "I have to teach an English lesson. Would you excuse me?" I say, "Why don't you let me teach the English lesson?" I am in Tajikistan illegally, trying to cross into the fighting in Afghanistan. But first I must get through the fighting in Tajikistan.

Hamrakul is a mountain guide, part-time English teacher, former prison guard in a Siberian gulag, and all-around mellow fellow. Naturally their are not many tourists here, and there is even less call for English teaching in this Tajik/Russian town. Consequently Hamrakul has never met any English-speaking people except for tourists. He learned English from reading books and then looking up the words he didn't know in a dictionary. His pronunciation is flawless but there are massive gaps in his vocabulary. I discover why. He likes pulp crime novels, has read *Moby-Dick* eight times and *Shall We Tell the President* ten times. He sits with me in the café and apologizes for his drunk friends. As we chat I learn that I am in the home of backgammon, a fifth-century Sogdian game, here called *nard*. I also learn that the national game of Tajikistan is *shahmot,* or chess. *Shahmot* means "blocked king." Tajikistan is also the birthplace of wheat and the pea. I just learned more about Tajikistan in five minutes than in the last two months of preparation.

I met Hamrakul on a tour bus I snuck in on, wealthy country counters making a day tour from Samarkand into Pendjikent. The attraction was an ancient Sogdian city but the real purpose was to add one more country to the hundred-plus most of them have visited. I bade them good-bye at the end of the day and found myself in a cold, war-torn country without a word of Russian or any idea of how I would navigate the forbidding mountain pass that separated me from my destination.

Hamrakul and I trot off to the school. On the way an extremely drunk man slams into me. Then he flicks his neck with his finger and thumb and starts punching me in the arm. He holds onto my other arm to keep from falling into the street. Hamrakul says, "I am sorry for him, but he wants you to drink with him." I try to explain that he has a head start on me, so maybe tomorrow when we can start together would be better. Despite the gentle protestations of Hamrakul, the man won't let go. Frustrated that Hamrakul is trying to pry away his new drinking buddy, he starts hammering my friend, who is half the size of me and not likely to survive too much abuse. I don't know what to do because Hamrakul then explains that this is one of his best friends and fellow teachers. (I find out later he teaches health and physical fitness.) So we continue to walk down the street being punched and yelled at until finally he forgets what he is doing, wheels like an ape, and staggers off in the opposite direction.

There are two young girls waiting for us at the school. The boys haven't bothered showing up. We wait patiently for over an hour and a half for the other students to arrive, then I spend about an hour teaching two girls their first English lesson. At the end of the lesson they are talking to me in gently accented English. I still can't speak a word of Russian or Tajik. I am both humbled and gratified.

At age three, I already have a penchant for nicely cut suits.

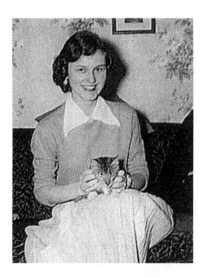

My mother-to-be, 1954.

On a school break at age nine with my brother, age six.

At age eleven in a familiar pose: with my father and an airplane.

Advertisement for St. John's teachers.

Seaside home on Hollywood Crescent in Victoria, B.C.

At age fourteen.

Age nineteen in Colombia.

Age twenty on the Yukon border.

*Putting together the 5,120 slides and miles of film
for "The Great Toronto Adventure."*

California living.

*From this suit, you'd never guess I was
actually a tunneler.*

Twins.

*Linda had them for nine months,
then I got to play mother.*

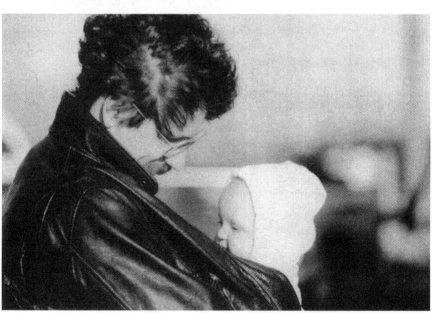

Like a lion with his cubs.

Camel Trophy, Burundi. Four men in a soaking wet, filthy truck for two weeks. Words fail me . . .

This is how you get across when they forget to build bridges.

That night we share dinner at Hamrakul's simple apartment. (Although he is pushing fifty, he and his extended family live in his mother's apartment.) There is no hesitation in him inviting me to stay. The pompadoured guide whom I call Elvis has returned from escorting the bus to the border and cracks open a bottle of local wine, a passable sherry they pour into their own bottles directly from the factory up the road. In any Russian or former Russian country you don't sip booze, you slam it. Conversations are punctuated with toasts to health, your host, and later on in the evening to vaguer concepts like life and friendship and then, finally, just drinking.

We talk about life under the Russians and now. They are nostalgic. Under the Russians things worked, the planes flew, there was petrol for the cars and there were jobs. Now there is nothing. But— Elvis laughs loudly—"The Russians taught us how to drink!" Another toast and we are on our third bottle.

They tell me a joke:

A Frenchman, an Englishman, and a Russian are on a desert island. They release a genie in a bottle who grants each one a wish. The Frenchman and Brit demand to be sent home into the arms of their loved ones along with mountains of riches. The Russian ponders his choice and after a while exclaims he would like two cases of vodka and . . . "for his friends to come back to drink them with him."

I am starting to think that the Tajiks miss the Russians.

I learn about the tourism business in this part of Tajikistan. Hamrakul is a freelance guide but Elvis is a tour operator. Elvis must pay the equivalent of $5,000 for a license and then $3,000 a year to be current. If you want to go climbing, you pay $100 for an ascent over six thousand meters and trekkers pay $1 a day for an "ecology" tax. There are a few people who come to climb mountains but news of war has kept them away. Here there is no war and never has been a war. But still it keeps the people away.

I ask how I can get to Dushanbe, the Tajik capital. There are no planes, trains, buses, or other regular transport. There is very little fuel and what is available is sold in glass jars at the side of the road. They say the only way is to find a car and negotiate. If you wait down by where the buses are, maybe you can find some other people who want to go. Local people pay about sixty dollars per car, so it depends on how many people you can stuff inside. That's if you can find a driver who wants to take the treacherous trip and anyone else who wants to go.

"Treacherous?" I ask.

It seems there are ten military roadblocks, washed-out roads, landslides, smashed wooden bridges, and a 3,700-meter-high mountain pass between me and Dushanbe. A measure of the difficulty is made clear when Hamrakul tells me that it is dangerous enough that he hasn't visited his cousin in Dushanbe for six years.

I offer to pay for Hamrakul's passage and his return if he will accompany me and tell me more about Tajikistan. He says he must ask his wife and will tell me in the morning, for now he is drunk and cannot think. Elvis says that he, too, is very drunk and should be leaving. He will find his driver to take him home. Hamrakul reminds him that there is no one outside and it is very cold. Elvis assures us that he will find his way as he staggers down the stairs jabbing and groping to find the armhole in his jacket. Before we bed down for the night Hamrakul says we will be okay if it does not rain tonight. I don't know if he is talking about Elvis passing out and freezing to death or the mountain pass being snowed in.

I, too, am drunk and must sleep, but first I ask Hamrakul what it was like to work in a gulag. He just says he went into the army and was a prison guard in a Siberian gulag. That's it. All he wants to say about that phase of his life is that the prisoners ate and lived in conditions better than he did. He shows me his Russian passport which by law must have a new photograph every fifteen years. In his youth he was a dapper, handsome man. In his fifties he is a hard, sad man.

He looks at my passport. "Time has been kinder to you."

THE GRAND PORTAGE

Thunder Bay, Ontario · The voyageurs of eighteenth-century North America were adventurers, rugged and short-lived. They lived in a vast wilderness defined only by mercenary grants to trading companies like the Hudson's Bay Company and the North West Company. Typically they were French, often the product of lonely unions between Indian squaws and French settlers. The toughest were the Northmen, or *hivernauts* (winterers), who lived in what is now the Canadian Northwest. They trapped and traded with Indians, gathering the beaver pelts in vogue in Europe and America. In winter they traveled by snowshoe, relying on self-sufficiency and enterprise to gather their goods for the spring trade. To be hired as a voyageur for one of the two trading companies, they had to be under five feet six to avoid stealing precious cargo space.

When the ice broke in the spring, they made their way to the regional trading forts at Rocky Mountain House, Winnipeg, and Fort Churchill and began canoeing.

The hierarchy of each canoe was simple and based on experience. The leader was the *gouvernail,* or steersman, who directed the actions of the *avant* (bowsman) and the *milieux* (middle men). They carried traders or *bourgeois* who were granted the privilege of being carried to and from the canoe so they wouldn't get their feet wet. The men lived hard lonely lives during the winter and enjoyed this annual gathering and voyage, eating simple food and sleeping under their overturned canoes. Although much is made of the carousing, happy image of the voyageurs, they were also subject to depression, drunkenness, loneliness, fighting, suicide, and the constant pressure of the competing fur companies. They sang songs to maintain the speed of the stroke and fight the fear of the thundering waters. They played an Indian game called *la crosse* and a tug-of-war game between canoes designed to dump the loser in the frigid water.

In voyageur days the Grand Portage was the Everest of its time. A man could measure his worth and accomplishments by how many times he had done the Grand Portage. This nine-mile trail separated the real voyageur from the city slicker who came across the Great Lakes to trade at Fort William.

In its naiveté the school had tried this route the year before but had used the large four-hundred-pound canoes and eight men. They liked to use the term "men" when describing the young teens that accompanied the out-of-shape "masters." They forgot that a canvas canoe with wooden frame absorbs water until it becomes a leaden beast almost double its dry weight. The painful push through swamps and up hills redirects all four hundred pounds to the shortest boy and drives the skinny victim into the mud like a sledgehammer pounding a nail. The older crews that had tried the Grand Portage with the great freighter canoes the year before had started at two in the afternoon and by eight that night they were only four and a half miles in. They didn't get to the other end of the portage until the following day. It took them forty-four hours. So much for bad math and false encouragement.

The year we attempted it, it was decided to use the smaller, 240-pound canoes and four "men" to carry them. These men included twelve- and thirteen-years-olds and one eleven-year-old: me. And once again the teacher's math skills let them down because although eight men carrying the four-hundred-pound canoe came out to fifty pounds per person, a smaller canoe with fewer people put the weight at sixty pounds per child. Add to that the fifty to one hundred pounds of water and mud the canoes soaked up and each kid was shouldering at least eighty pounds over the nine-mile distance.

Before we left, we practiced by carrying sawed-off telephone poles. Then we just carried our canoes for miles at a time. The sharp edge of the gunnels cut and bent our shoulders until they were black with bruises. There is really no muscle or skill that can be developed to carry one to two hundred pounds of canoe on your shoulder. You just hope you don't let your teammates down, because it would be physically impossible for three children to carry a dry canoe, let alone a waterlogged one.

Nine miles is not a long distance on a map, but it can be a life-scarring experience when it's walked by children carrying a canoe, particularly when much of the way is a corduroy road of old rotting logs through mosquito-filled swamps. The mosquitoes torment you, hunger and thirst annoy you, the sweat runs down your face and stings your eyes. Often your teammates have to pull you out of the mud because the weight of the canoe has driven you in deeply, like a tent peg. Some kids, brought face-to-face with pain and the futility of the exercise, started giving up. Much violent discussion would then ensue until the victim was convinced to carry his corner, sobbing, until he tripped or collapsed. By the fourth or fifth mile the woods were full of children screaming in pain and crying. It was a strange sound, something like a wounded animal, except these were cries of brutality, rage, and frustration. Even those who had the fortitude to carry on were crying. By the late afternoon we were all just taking it a few feet at a time. Some of the crews had given up, others had gone back to replace missing members. Rumor had it that someone ran into the dense woods to escape.

I would imagine that many people have done the Grand Portage, and a handful enjoyed it. Later that year the school would brag about the first team of thirteen- and fourteen-year-old boys making the nine-mile run in three hours and forty minutes. They did it by walking for ten minutes, resting, and then walking again. Back in the rear, where things were much less noble, I spent my time doubling up to help the last crew. They did not get in until the following morning. When I remember it, I think of the words of the coroner: "an exaggerated and pointless adventure." Yet somehow, late that moonless night, we stumbled into a clearing and heard the sound of the Pigeon River. We had just started our trip.

My canoe would not make it. One day our steersman took the

wrong tributary against our advice and plunged us into a maelstrom of white water and rocks. In the distance I could see a telltale line of mist. I could also feel the change in pressure that foretells a great fall of water. We were headed over a thirty-foot waterfall. As our speed increased, there was little we could do. At the last minute we paddled for a V between two rocks. Mercifully the bow of the canoe wedged between them and we stuck fast. There we stayed, the water too fast for anyone to venture out of the boat and we too occupied trying to prevent the rear from catching the water and spinning us around to do anything else.

After a very long time the other crews figured out what had happened to us. With ropes and much nervous tension we built a hand-hold from the canoe to the shore and then skittered and surfed to safety, abandoning the canoe we had worked so hard to bring this far. Windblown, exhausted, and running out of food and time, we called it quits two hundred miles short of the thousand-mile goal of Selkirk.

Later that year they pulled out our canoe from its rocky perch above the waterfall, but it was too bent from the pressure and beating of the fast water to be much good. I, too, was bent from the fast water and continual beating.

DOWN ON THE BORDER

Dushanbe, Tajikistan · I had made it. But now visaless, and having bade good-bye to my guide, I was on my own, hiding out in the only hotel in town. Down at breakfast I hand in my food chit and get a greasy sausage, pierogis, grapes, and Tajik bread. I see the other tourists. One is a large fiftyish woman and the other is a young man with the looks of an East German Stazi, complete with long leather coat and small pinched glasses. We sit at separate tables, each in our own world.

After breakfast I sit in the lobby and make some notes. The woman I had seen at breakfast comes up and asks if I am a journalist. I say no, I am just traveling and trying to get south to the Afghanistan border. She is a Swedish journalist and is traveling to the south with the United Nations this morning. She needs a photographer to cover the refugees returning from the fighting in Afghanistan Synchronicity is a big part of travel. It seems I am to become a photojournalist for the next few days.

The man I mistook for a Stazi agent is in fact a New Yorker and a field officer for the United Nations. Shows how well my judgment of character is working. Not only is he going to the south but he has read my book cover-to-cover and is thrilled that I have shown up.

We have lunch with folks from the United Nations High Commissioner for Refugees (UNHCR) behind their steel-gated compound. My UN host, Jonathan, has a degree in geology and a master's in intercultural management. He has just come from Herat, Afghanistan, and is here to help with the repatriation of thousands of refugees back from the war zone while things are calm in Mazar-e Sharif. He has an apartment for about $300 a month but spends most of his time down south in Shartuz. He makes around eighty grand a year plus subsistence pay, hazardous-duty pay, and tax incentives. He salts most of it away and figures by the time he is fifty he will have about half a million. The concept of making your "bundle" is strong motivation in the United Nations. But I sense that there is something more than money to encourage someone to work in Afghanistan and Tajikistan.

We are in a hurry to meet a train with about 310 refugees on board. After loading up our white UN Land Cruiser, we drive at breakneck speed through the war zone. The Tajik refugees have come from Mazar by truck, barge, and train and will be off-loaded, fed, and then sent off with their goods to their bombed and shattered villages. There have been casualties from the fighting and no one knows what kind of condition the refugees will be in.

Down near the southern border I arrive in a Sergio Leone movie tableau. In a land that is brown and sparse there is a single building, a water tower, and an ancient, dilapidated Russian train. The pale blue sky and the dry hills beyond frame the scene perfectly.

This group of refugees has been waiting five years to come home. The children are covered with sores and the people are tired and dirty. Men break down and cry in their relatives' arms as they welcome them back. It is a touching scene and one that reinforces the UN's purpose. Without the intervention of the United Nations these people would never be able to leave Afghanistan, cross through Uzbekistan, and rebuild their lives again.

It seems the Uzbek police who were charged with the security of the refugees were actually stealing and looting the refugees' possessions piled in open cars at the back of the train as the Tajiks watched helplessly from the passenger cars in front. The Uzbek police threw possessions to their friends waiting at the side of the tracks at a predetermined bend.

Demanding that I photograph the proof of this crime, the Tajiks hold up slashed bags, empty cases, and smashed goods. I suddenly feel like I have a purpose and I lose track of Jonathan. Later I find him sitting in his truck with the doors locked, screaming on the radio at the top of his voice. He is frustrated by the bureaucracy; the head office is reassigning his people to other areas and he is expected to squire around a German delegation. Meanwhile he is also expected, along with three others, to get 310 people fed, housed, and organized in a few hours. Each person will get one 50-kilogram sack of flour, 2.4 kilograms of sugar, 3.6 kilograms of cooking oil, one plastic sheet, and one blanket. Only the flour comes in the right-size container. Jonathan must calculate how much will be needed on each night and in each place, organize the arrival and transportation of nine carloads of personal goods, and then organize a fleet of trucks to take each family with their goods to the right village. At night he must fill out the appropriate forms, monitor budgets, and assign personnel to make sure he has enough resources. Coordinating workers, chasing down thieves, stacking up the next shipments, talking on the radio to headquarters, planning tomorrow's massive unloading, setting up security, even figuring how to divide all the wrong-size cooking-oil containers into the UN-mandated ration sizes, Jonathan is in his element. Late into the night, he says it is hard, lonely work but worth it. I'm thinking that's exactly what he is supposed to say to journalists.

The next day we return to the lonely rail station. It is chaos. Tons of personal effects are scattered around the rail line as each person tries to coordinate with an open-bed truck that will take them to their village. I take pictures for the Swedish journalist, Disa, who is doing an article on the refugees. Men pose proudly with their chickens. Not quite knowing why they deserve celebrity, they stop and stand straight as boards for their pictures. Relatives still come to search out long-lost loved ones, and in between the industry there are tearful reunions and prayers for deliverance.

We accompany some of the families returning to their deserted villages. In the ruins people are making mud bricks and rebuilding their homes. There is a different feeling now. The people are happy as they sit on their blue plastic sheets and rebuild their lives. "This is the part that makes it all worthwhile," says Jonathan. I know he means it.

Shortly after I left, two French aid workers were kidnapped in Tajikistan. Eventually the gunmen let the male worker go and kept the female. In response to this the government got tough, showing up with a tank outside the house where the female hostage was being held. The gunmen walked outside, with the hostage, holding a grenade, and, in a show of defiance, pulled the pin. They all died.

GRISTLE GOES LIGHTLY

Victoria, British Columbia · I had spent a rudderless two years in Toronto living with my father. When I came out of St. John's, "flower power" was in full effect. Long hair, Nehru jackets, drugs, do your thing. I knew nothing about music, movies, girls, or even what teenagers were supposed to do.

My father worked during the day and would sit comfortably at night with a glass of rye whiskey and a pack of cigarettes. He never smoke or drank during the day. Next to him were tall stacks of airplane magazines neatly folded to articles he read and reread. My brother and I didn't do much. We hung out together, rode our bikes, snuck onto the air force base across the street, but generally stayed in our rooms. On weekends we would go flying with my father. He loved aerobatics and we would sit in the back of the plane as we flew to various air shows. I learned to fly but had no interest in getting a license. On the weekends that my father was busy I would take the subway to the international airport and watch the planes take off. I did poorly in school because I just didn't care. In a strange coincidence my school was named after the great illustrator C. W. Jeffries, who drew scenes of the voyageurs and trappers. I never bothered telling my classmates how intimately I knew that life.

Then one day my mother called to ask if we could spend the summer in Victoria. Memories flooded back and we went, packing a little suitcase and promising to be back in time for school.

We were met at the airport by a beaming mother driving a classic gray Jaguar 3.4. She was shocked at our pimpled, unkempt, gangly look. On the way home she bought fresh flowers and talked excitedly about our new life together. She had married her former boss, a geologist named Donald. Within the first week she sat us down and asked us if we wanted to live with her for good. Her rationale was that now that she was happily married and settled down we could all live happily ever after. I believed her because I wanted to believe her. We would live in her apartment on the ocean and start school in Victoria that fall.

My two years in high school were my flowering. I began to get involved in school affairs, made movies, paid people to eat worms and then charged admission, started the outdoors club. I wrote an award-winning radio show for an American station in Washington State, was on the student council, bicycled across the mountains of British Columbia, rebuilt a car, mastered photography, and even started to do well at school. There was nothing that could stop me in any physical or mental task. Despite being much younger than most of my classmates, I felt like I belonged.

When I entered my twelfth and final grade of school, my friends began to make plans for college and I began to ask my parents about what my plans might be. This met with stony silence. I was bubbling with plans to hike to a remote rain forest preserve up-island, travel to Europe, go to college, get a summer job, and just be normal. The day after the graduation ceremony my mother turned to me and said, "Donald and I have decided it's time for you to leave home." I was sixteen and homeless.

PART TWO

EVOLUTION

THE QUEEN OF KING CITY

King City, California · It's time to take another high-speed motorcycle tour. Like a fly fisher who fishes and relishes the same stream, I must look within the obvious to see if I can understand the nuances of my own life.

A stiff northern headwind forces us to stay in King City. King City is famous for nothing except maybe being the speeding-ticket capital of California. On the streets Mexican cowboys strut in that tight-crotched-walk that freshly washed jeans create. They are done up in their best finery: crisp black hats, tight black jeans, and white embroidered shirts. They have a hard, sunburned, chiseled look Clint Eastwood would envy.

It is Friday night. The work in the fields is done and the money has been Western Unioned back to family in Mexico. Every worker carefully counts out his money for a night on the town. They could buy a twenty-four pack and stay at home but it's lonely in King City at the dusty edge of the onion fields and there are women here in the bar.

I assume from their looks and language that the girls are from Mexico until suddenly one of the taller, drunker ones leans back and yells, "Are you a good fuck?" It seems the girl in the white hot pants is not a transplanted Mexican but is from Nebraska. She gets twenty dollars for a blow job in the men's bathroom; the other girls only get five. From my crude timing of her comings and goings to the john, I calculate she averages about five minutes a customer. She is on something, something cheap, painful, and ultimately deadly. Her head weaves out of rhythm with her eyes, like she's on a carnival ride and can't synchronize.

"Two kids." She pulls up her blouse to show me her stretch marks the same way a vet will show you a bullet wound. "I love sex." Or so she tells me. She got married on a cruise ship in Hawaii. She was married for three years and left him. He has three houses, a car, and a boat. She drops in and out of her story line depending on whether the alcohol or the speed is kicking in. It seems my dispassionate gaze is bringing back bad memories. "You're a cop. I'll sue your ass off for harassment." She is in her own painful world. She can't break through.

"How well do you fuck?" she demands again, drunkenly, not expecting an answer. It's an insult, an attempt to shock. Like a rock thrown at a new dress behind the store window. Her eyes flash. All the men watch her. She knows it. Here she is the queen, the most beautiful girl in the King City sports bar.

She tells me she wants to die on top of someone, that she can't remember whether she hates me or needs me. She has said this before, probably each time she gets arrested. Suddenly realizing she is saying far too much, she gets up and takes another stranger to the bathroom.

A cherub-faced American walks into the bar, as out of place in his Gap gear as an aborigine on Wall Street. He's in that coming-up-to-middle-age overweight place where success bumps into complacency. He is nervous at first and then suddenly happy to see two white faces among the hard, suntanned Mexicans.

"Hey, gringos, you guys speak my language. Don't people tell you you look just like Mel Gibson?" he says to Wink. We name him the Dove Hunter because he comes here from San Francisco to go dove hunting every year. Somebody told him that there are girls here, so he thought he would hang out and see for himself.

The Dove Hunter from San Francisco will say, "Hey, this is fucking great," many times during the evening. He loves to hear our stories about the girl in white who is sitting just three feet away. Somehow it sounds better secondhand. He could just lean over and ask her himself but there is something dangerous about that woman, something that keeps him facing us instead of her.

Two thick-necked cops appear by the washrooms and when I look around for the girl in white she is gone. I'm relieved because I know why she hurts. But she is mortally wounded, I survived. By midnight I have drunk too much. Carefully I make my way back to where I should be, among the neon lights and drive-through signs near the freeway.

I notice two things: the fields come up to the edge of town, and the smell of onions is pervasive and warm.

ON THE ROAD

Victoria, British Columbia · I was out on the streets in less than a week. The fact that it came just before my seventeenth birthday was no coincidence; it was a conclusion that had probably been reached months before. And like the best professional hits, I had walked right up to my executioner.

Walking by a used-car lot, I saw a car with a sale price of $175. It was a 1962 Rambler station wagon that was pink and "Pullmanized," which means the car folded into a flat bed-like surface. I bought it for $150 on the spot. My brother decided that he would rather be with me, so together we headed out in our high-mileage Rambler to explore the world.

Living in a car is now called being homeless. When you're sixteen, it's called being on vacation. Together we explored every road on my British Columbia tourist map. We lived on peanut butter sandwiches and bathed by swimming in Lake Okanogan. When the police would roust us at night, I would tell them we were camping. When I ran out of money, my brother and I picked fruit in the Okanogan Valley. We lived in rat-infested workers' huts as we picked pears and peaches. We were paid by the six-by-six-foot box and it often took both of us a whole day just to make five or ten dollars.

After a while the idea of driving aimlessly seemed pointless and I phoned my mother to ask her what the hell possessed her to kick me out. Her words were "It's time for you to become a man." If I remembered correctly, that's what she said I'd become when I was ten.

The weather soon turned cold and I couldn't spend my life living in a car. I headed east to stay with my father until I could figure out what I wanted to do with the rest of my life. The Rambler got me across the country, but just. Before I reached Toronto I was pouring in quarts of 80-weight oil to get me about a hundred miles before the red oil light would come on. My car and my ambition could take me no farther. I felt like Adam chased out of paradise.

DANCING WITH THE HEADHUNTERS

Somewhere along the Rajang River, Sarawak · I am the American part of a multinational expedition through Sarawak, and part of our cultural responsibility is to spend a night in this remote longhouse. We have heard horror stories of these tourist shows, of how the drinking and dancing are more for the benefit of the inhabitants than the guests— sort of an orgiastic prelude to a garage sale. The members of our expedition from Sarawak told me I could always just roll over and go to sleep if the gongs got too tedious. They lied.

There are over fifteen hundred longhouses to choose from in Sarawak, and all of their habitants will offer Dayak hospitality if their graciousness is primed with gifts or moldy *ringgits* (cash). We chose a remote longhouse on the Skrang River where there were many elders and a mixture of Muslim, Christian, and animist dwellers that still carried on in relative shelter from karaoke bars, ghetto blasters, and old Abba tapes. It was also on the Skrang River that Sir James Brooke massacred over eight hundred Ibans in 1849. Now it appears it is pay-back time. But before I begin it's important to understand just what and who an Iban is.

The Skrang River is now the traditional home of the Iban people. This area was first settled by Ibans between the sixteenth and eighteenth centuries. Their proximity to the ocean earned them the name "Sea Dayaks" as opposed to Land Dayaks, the typically more sedate Bidayuhs, Kayans, and Kenyahs, who lived farther upriver. The Ibans originally settled on the Kapuas River basin in central Borneo. They have a very distinct culture and look, and are probably the most famous of the Dayaks.

Despite their touristic ambitions, the Ibans are among my favorite peoples.

It wasn't until about a hundred years ago, when Westerners promoted the concept of education, that the Ibans developed a written form of communication. Before then, like most Dayaks of Borneo, they had no written language, passing down their history and culture through oral recitation of events. Like many indigenous tribes, they used a singsong rhythm to help them remember the lengthy tales. According to this oral history, the Ibans came from the Indonesian island of Java and from the north, in what is now Cambodia. They settled in Sabah around Marudu Bay. Intense raids by the Sulu islanders from the Philippines forced them south to the town now called Bintulu in Sarawak. The sultan of Brunei then forced them to Sambas in what is now Kalimantan.

The Ibans were industrious, gathered wealth, and were trading with the Majapahits in Java. When the government fell, the Ibans fled into north-central Borneo, but afraid that they would be under the control of another tribe, they decided to move to new ground. They had not yet learned how to build dugout canoes and their rafts broke apart in the fast river waters. In frustration they moved overland. Later migrations took them to the head of the Kapuas River. Further migrations took them up the Skrang and Padih Rivers. When the

British came, they referred to the Ibans as Sea Dayaks, and it was with these entrepreneurial fighters that James Brooke formed an alliance to push back marauding pirates.

The Ibans are legendary hosts; an Iban will always house and feed a visitor without question. They love to venture into the unknown; an unadventurous Iban male is referred to as a *batu tungku,* which is their word for the resting stone in a fireplace. Men are expected to travel and test their ability to survive and overcome adversity. Ibans are also very honest. They are known to always tell the truth. Accordingly, theft is rare and any Iban caught lying or stealing is reminded of it for the rest of his or her life.

Just as the Kenyahs are known for their rigid social structure, the Ibans are known for their classless, democratic society. Their appreciation and creation of artistic motifs and culture is second only to the Kenyahs' and Kayans'. The Ibans are probably most famous for their escalation of headhunting from a cultural necessity to recreation.

The most dramatic and visible symbol of Iban culture is the longhouse. The longhouse is the precursor of the town home: fifteen to twenty houses joined together and built on stilts. The original longhouses were much higher off the ground, with notched logs that were pulled up at night for security. The modern longhouses are rebuilt many times, each time getting slightly lower to the ground. Everything that is foul or needs to be discarded is simply dropped to the ground below. Only the brave dare look under a longhouse.

There is one long common area in front of the homes, and in front of each house is a collection of blackened human skulls. Most of the skulls date back to World War II when the Japanese gave freely of their craniums. Nowadays the skulls serve the same purpose as jockeys on suburban lawns: they are relics of days gone by. Strangely enough, the heads bring prosperity to the longhouses. In Sarawak the more heads, the more tourists.

We arrive at the longhouse tired and dirty. Although we are four hours late, our hosts tell us the party is just beginning. As we enter at one end of the longhouse, we notice a live pig tied up and we are invited to dispatch the evening's main course using a proffered spear; the party always commences with the traditional killing of a pig.

Needless to say, the pig is about as happy with this custom as we are, but old traditions die hard. In this case, so did the pig. As he is being shoved over to the side to contemplate his skewered state, we follow a group of dancing headmen preceded by musicians playing the traditional gong music. While the pig's eyes glaze over and his blood soaks into the warm ground, we enter the longhouse and begin to make our rounds. As we pass each front door of the twenty-odd homes that make up the longhouse, we are offered a drink of *tuak*, homemade moonshine that would probably do wonders as nail polish remover.

Drinking *tuak* isn't the hard part, it's trying *not* to drink the stuff by the time you get to the twentieth house that's difficult. In this case, our hosts are so excited to be the recipients of such a grand delegation, they decide to take us around the longhouses again and again until only white sediment shows at the bottom of the recycled whiskey bottles. So far so good. I am twenty minutes into experiencing a longhouse for the first time and I am drunk as a skunk.

At this point, almost deaf from the gong music and our heads spinning from the *tuak*, our hosts invite us to partake in another Iban tradition, bathing. The accumulation of dirt and sweat from our journey quickly disappears in the Skrang River that flows nearby. Skinny-dipping by the light of the full moon, we hope that any waterborne predators will be repulsed by the amount and quality of dirt with which we are polluting the river. It is a magical feeling to be waist-deep in the cool water, the moonlight making silvery wobbles off the black water and, in the distance, the warm glow of candles and Coleman lanterns shining through the chinks in the wooden longhouse. The gong music fades in and out and the high-pitched chatter of native women sounds an evocative note. They are watching us and giggling. We don't feel embarrassed, since we are eager to adopt the traditions of the noble savage. Later I am told that men and women never bathe nude but always wear some type of sarong or covering. Suddenly I get a shiver, not from the fish that keep bumping against my private parts, but from the fragment I remember reading about Iban headhunting—how the night of the full moon was ideal for taking heads while men bathed, their weapons left in the longhouse.

Back inside, cool and refreshed, the night begins in earnest. The evening feast consists of round after round of *tuak,* rice, and a wide variety of well-cooked, chewy jungle animals. Our newly deceased pig reappears as chunks of greasy, barbecued pork. To aid in our digestion, there are speeches—not just one but many. As a matter of fact, one speech from every senior member of the longhouse. The speeches are in the Iban dialect, so it sounds like somebody listing electrical parts with great importance. Since the members of the expedition are from Sweden, Turkey, Germany, France, Japan, the United States, and Australia, we respond in kind with long-winded speeches in our own languages. Naturally our guests do not understand one word but applaud wildly. Then we give gifts. I take Polaroids of the headman and present them with a great flourish. I pass out baseball cards to the children and little trinkets to the women. Although I feel like I am negotiating a land deal, their genuine look of thanks is heartwarming.

By midnight the food is cleared and we are ready for more dancing and drinking. The residents of the longhouse don the ceremonial headdress of hornbill feathers and grasp a fierce, razor-sharp knife, essentially a homemade machete with a deer antler handle and a decorative sheath. They dance in turn for the entertainment of their guests. After displaying their prowess, they proceed to drag protesting members of the audience out into the dance floor and challenge them to display their talents.

There are not a lot of impressive dance steps that can be choreographed to a sound track that is a cross between banging hubcaps and a car crash, but try we do. Luckily the *tuak* removed any inhibitions we might have had and we play to our audience. The "funky chicken," the "mashed potato," whatever we choose they can't get enough of it. They laugh and laugh and laugh.

As we get more exhausted, they seem to pick up speed. In between goofy foreign dances the Ibans do imitations of us, which inspires us to do imitations of them. By 4:00 A.M. we notice a thinning in the foreign contingent. Realizing that we stalwart few are nearing exhaustion, our hosts search out the poor unfortunates who had sneaked off to the far reaches of the longhouse to sleep. Without missing a beat they crack open their mouths, pour in an invigorating slug of coconut wine, then lead them onto the dance floor for more entertainment.

Close to dawn, I stagger to a dark corner of the longhouse to catch a few winks of sleep. Collapsing on the wood floor, I feel hands under my head. My eyes flick open in the blue dawn and I see a woman putting a pillow under my head. Around her are the silhouettes of her family squatting, chatting softly. I drift back to sleep, and an hour later the strident roosters under the longhouse wake me. I now have a blanket on me. The family are still there, chatting softly. They see that I am awake and invite me to share their simple breakfast with them. As I get ready to leave, I give them whatever useful items are in my bag and wish them luck. The Ibans did not take my head but my heart.

THE MAILBOY

Toronto, Ontario · To determine what industry should be blessed by my talents, a counselor back in Victoria had suggested that I take an aptitude and interest test. Being somewhat familiar with the testing process, I didn't hold much faith in the results. The aptitude test told me that I was in the top 5 to 1 percentile of the population in a number of skills, including language, spatial relations, and communications. The things that won't get you a job. I was in the lowest 20th percentile in things like math and other hard sciences where the money was. When the results of my "interests" were put together with my "skills," there were only three jobs I would be good at: astronaut, adventurer, and advertising man.

I determined that I would try my luck at the third choice: advertising. My job-seeking skills weren't sophisticated. I looked under "Advertising" in the Yellow Pages and started calling. When asked who I wanted to talk to, I read the name that was listed in the phone book. After several instances of being politely informed that the founder of the company had died fifty years ago, or that that long name was actually three people, I just started asking for the president. When asked what my business was, I said, "I took a test in high school that said I should be an advertising man, so I'm calling about a job."

Despite my brashness, I did speak to a number of presidents. Many of them invited me to come by and see them after work. They showed me award-winning commercials, took me on tours around their elegant offices, and some even asked me what I would do if I were to rewrite one of their ads. For the first time I knew exactly what I wanted. Advertising sounded glamorous, exciting, and a good way to use my talents. I could write, draw, take pictures, strategize, make films, be creative, and even write jingles. It also seemed that smart, creative, funny people worked in the business . . . and they were paid a lot of money. It didn't take long for me to decide that advertising was my life's ambition.

The other compelling aspect of advertising was that you didn't need a university degree to get a job. One of the common denominators of the executives I met seemed to be that they had started just like me: young, eager, and at the bottom. We all agreed that advertising was made for me and I was made for advertising.

Since we were in complete agreement, my response was "Great, then give me a job." It was then that I learned two things. One is that you need experience to get a job and the other is that you need a job to get experience. I had swept floors, ground the little extra bits off of Styrofoam Santa Claus boots, and picked fruit, but none of those were considered sufficient experience to be a copywriter. One august corporate head advised me to start in the mail room like he did. I thanked him and marched straight down to the mail department the next day to get my job. They wanted to know how much experience I had delivering mail. Sorry, no job.

This sent me on a quest to become a mailboy, the most aggressive, sharpest, fastest damn mailboy that ever existed. I soon found a job at Merrill Lynch, the stockbrokers. Within a couple of weeks not only had I revolutionized the concept and speed of mail delivery but I was also reading every single document, letter, report, magazine, and newspaper that came through our little cubbyhole.

Within a week I knew all the accounts, who was trading what, what the corporate priorities and plans were, who thought what of whom, and I enjoyed discussing it at length with the senior executives every time I would drop their mail off. At the end of the month when we mailed out the statements, I would read every one to see which stocks and which investors did well. I bummed the traders' training manuals from the brokers' floor, knew the names of all the key players, and could even tell you what any stock was trading for at that time and whether it would rise or fall. I quickly made plenty of successful investments and became a multimillionaire but unfortunately only on paper. I had no money to buy any real stocks and my paper empire impressed no one.

Needless to say, it wasn't long before my supervisor took me aside and told me that he had been asked by someone very high up to fire me. It seemed that the executives did not look kindly on a mere mailboy discussing the finer points covered in their private correspondence. My sage advice on how to solve internal problems, expand business, and increase profitability was also unwanted. My job was to open the mail, sort it, and deliver it. Period.

Thankfully I was given another chance because my boss admired my enthusiasm. He was a man in his late forties whose long spell in the mail room gave meaning to his caution on the realities of lower-echelon white-collar living. If I did my job too quickly, I would make the other people look slow. If I continually brought up ways to make mail delivery efficient, then I made him look bad. If we become too efficient and needed less staff, he would have less importance.

I got the point.

One day an ad appeared in the paper for a mailboy at an ad agency. The next day I took a long lunch and presented myself as God's gift to mail distribution with special skills as it relates to advertising.

A SECRET RENDEZVOUS

Kalimantan, Indonesia · It's two and a half hours by boat to Long Ampung, a sleepy town in the highlands of Indonesian Borneo where chickens walk slowly, dogs sleep like the dead, and the wind is too lazy to move. The neat government precision of Long Nawang, where my plane should have landed, contrasts with the randomly scattered layout of Long Ampung, where it crashed. It's a haphazard collection of ramshackle, run-down, unpainted houses and longhouses, sprawling on both sides of the river and connected by a suspension bridge pieced together with old pieces of wire, rattan, sticks, wood, and string.

Here, people seem to be marking time on a broken clock. The word "hillbilly" comes to mind. People say *"Selamat soreng"* for "Good afternoon," or just *"Soreng."* It sounds like they are saying "Sorry," as in "I'm sorry you're here." Missionaries dump all the abandoned T-shirts of the world here—Ninja turtles, Batman, films and fads that are long forgotten. The roads are wide in Long Nawang, but in Long Ampung there is only a thin, meandering dirt path scuffed into the middle of an overgrown clearing. People don't change direction much here.

I am directed to a large central house but it doesn't seem like anyone is here. As I peer over the raised open side of the front platform, a wizened old man with long floppy ears sticks his head out. His wrinkled, scrunched-up face and hunched-over stature remind me of someone: I am talking to a tattooed Indonesian Yoda.

Pemgpung Anya waves us in with his hand. He has heard about the plane. Word gets around pretty quick here. Our dramatic arrival will probably be the biggest news for the next decade. Coskun, Jon, and I need a place to bunk down before making our next move. We know the people are poor here, so we don't ask to be fed, just to lie down on the dry wooden floor. As we lay out our gear, Pemgpung asks where our rice is. We have no rice. Most people here travel with sacks of rice, tobacco, and basic tools. Our protestations that we have freeze-dried food fall on deaf ears. He hobbles to his rice barn and gets a large basket of rice, then picks some tapioca leaves and *pakus*, or fern shoots.

Pemgpung Anya (he is called Pemgpung and visitors call him Ping Pong) was born in 1912. He built houses for the Dutch in the 1950s. He used to walk for five months to the coast and back with the other villagers for salt, cotton, and household articles. Each man would carry a hundred pounds.

Having worked up a sweat, he gives the ingredients to his son's wife and invites us to *makan*, or eat. Even though we are cooking beef Bourguignon, fettuccine Alfredo, and various other freeze-dried specialties, he insists that we drop our pretense of having enough and eat his food. We give him a sample of our food. He politely holds it in his hand and then disappears into the back of the longhouse, probably to throw the disgusting-tasting stuff to the chickens. Meanwhile, we busy ourselves stuffing rice into the empty foil packets to give to the dogs later. When he returns, he looks at how much we have eaten and orders more. This time we grimly stuff down as much as we can under his watchful eye. He is proud of his daughter-in-law because she makes pure white rice, not a husk or dark grain to be found.

The walls of the headman's house are decorated with the traditional art of the Apo Kayan region: fantastic swirls that intertwine dragons, jars, tigers, tendrils, and other designs. When Pemgpung is quizzed on the origins of this art, he bluntly responds by saying that someone came by and painted it. All he knows is that the traditional bit is the jar in the middle and the tiger. The tiger is a Hindu symbol. Tigers are found on the Malay Peninsula. When he first painted his longhouse, Pak asked the Dutch to show him a tiger skin so that he could copy it. The tendrils are modified with modern images and symbols. I am fascinated by tribal artwork but perhaps in Indonesia I have arrived too late.

Since we are stuck here, I ask him if the villagers can show us their costumes and dance. He will find out but for now they are all at church. There are three churches: Protestant, Catholic, and Gospel, all within spitting distance of each other. Some of the people go to all three churches so they don't piss off the missionaries. After church a few of the villagers show us a selection of ill-fitting and crudely made Kenyah costumes. Their flip-flops and logoed T-shirts under crudely painted war shields make it look like a fifth grader's version of a night in a longhouse. I decline their offer to put on a "cultural show" for us at an exorbitant rate. They are miffed. Pemgpung is embarrassed. It is hard for him to tell us that the Kenyahs of his village now dance only for tourists' money; they no longer dance for heads or for harvest. We have come so far, to what I thought was a remote place, only to discover that missionaries and tourists have turned it inside out.

Pemgpung invites us to spend the evening chatting with him even though we can barely understand each other. He begins to talk in his soft singsong manner, occasionally putting his hand on our arm for emphasis or stopping to scare a rooster off the veranda. He tells us stories of hunting bears. He tells us to wait until the sun bear rears up because the spear will not penetrate its thick hump. He tells us how he kills a pig: send dogs to frighten it, then shove a spear through its shoulder into its heart. He tells of using his blowgun to kill the elusive deer. He acts out the parts we don't understand and even pantomimes the blowgun part. He goes out, gets his old blowgun, and shows me how to use it.

Pak's friend comes from next door bringing the poison used to rub on the bamboo darts. Pak explains the two kinds of poison used and how to mix them together. He even tells us to be careful not to prick our fingers once we put the poison on the darts. He tells us how the Kenyahs used to get their pockets picked when they went into town. Then they began putting sharpened bamboo splinters with poison in their top pockets in a piece of paper. The practice of bilking country bumpkins ended quickly. Suddenly he decides we must know how to make darts and dashes out of the longhouse.

He comes back breathless with a length of seasoned bamboo he has hacked from the jungle and begins to carve. As he carves, the years fall away. He hums a song to himself. Rapidly the three-inch-round bamboo becomes chopstick-sized sticks. He sharpens each one into a rounded, pointed dart.

When we bring out the video camera, a big smile comes across his weathered face. Slowly he begins stamping his feet in a gentle urgent rhythm. Then he begins chanting, bending his neck and back in the birdlike position of the Kenyah war dance. He is enchanted. He promises to tell us many stories that night.

He invites his friend to help him sing the old songs. We go into the back of the longhouse so the rest of the village cannot hear. He tells us they don't like him to do this, since the whole village likes to charge for shows. He begins to sing the talking songs that are the oral history of the Kenyahs. The songs are long and take a long time to finish but there is an insistent rhythm and a need for these stories to be told.

He then asks if he can dance for us. Since there are no instruments, each man takes turns singing the musical accompaniment while the other dances. Pemgpung pretends to play a *sambé,* an ancient Kenyah guitar. Looking like a fourteen-year-old doing his version of Jimi Hendrix, he imitates the sound of the *sambé* while he strums and frets all the notes on his imaginary guitar and his friend dances.

Between songs we play back the music for the entertainers to hear. They yip, stamp their feet, and sing in harmony with the music. "This is magic!" they insist, enjoying it to the fullest. It is a sight to see the old man, his elongated ears flapping below the high-tech stereo headphones, dancing and clapping his hands like a teenager as he relives the tales of his youth.

Late into the morning they finally turn to us and say, "That is all we have to sing."

THE JOURNEY

Toronto, Ontario · After prepping myself with mailboy experience at Merrill Lynch I answered an ad for a mailboy at an ad agency, Baker Lovick BBDO, a Canadian branch of the large U.S. agency. I got the job. Like most mail departments, it was staffed by bitter, failed men and eager climbers. At the end of my first day I nervously waited until I could meet the head of the creative department. Breathlessly I told him of my ambition to be a copywriter and showed him my portfolio.

I don't know what Bob McAlear saw in me but he took me under his wing. I spent long nights in his darkened office at the end of the hall. Most evenings it was just me and him. He chain-smoked and had a large ceramic ashtray. I had to be careful not to talk too vigorously or I would blow the ashes all over his desk.

Although I had made it quite clear to Bob that I was ready to start work as a copywriter at a moment's notice, the call never came. Whenever I checked in to see if my job was ready, he would advise me to be patient. So I set about voraciously consuming every bit of information that moved throughout the company as well as what came in the big canvas mailbags every morning. It seems that they were pitching a big account for a cookie manufacturer. Despite the repeated attempts of the creative department, nothing had clicked. I spent my weekends off visiting supermarkets, talking to housewives, and finding out how best to market this new product. I banged away on my father's old Remington, deliciously ignorant of any marketing or advertising strategies, and wrote a complete marketing plan including the creative proposal. Proudly I dumped it on Bob's desk and then heard nothing for a week. Soon I was starting to get dirty looks from the creative staff as I delivered their mail. Finally I asked a copywriter what was up. He told me a story.

They had held a meeting. In that meeting Bob went around the room asking each member of the creative and accounting staff how long they had spent working on this project and how much money they made.

He then handed out multiple copies of a proposal.

The people assembled around the table expressed their delight at this new solution. Bob then asked if anybody knew who had written it. They didn't. Finally Bob could contain himself no longer. "The fucking mailboy wrote this over the weekend. And do you know what we pay him? Less than a fucking dollar an hour!"

I become a trainee copywriter after that.

Bob was interesting not just because he was my boss's boss but because he was trying to do more than advertising. He had just won another award but not for his advertising creativity. He was the recipient of an award for his book on truth in advertising, something he had thought strongly about in the last few years. He felt that advertising was one of the most pervasive forms of entertainment and education and that its creators and practitioners had to be responsible for what they created. Bob had also gone back to school and received a doctorate in theology.

His lessons to me were never specific. He encouraged me to expand my vocabulary, to find the words that connected with people, to tell the truth, simply and with conviction. I thought I could do what he asked and I had an ear for what sounded right, to create words that sang, but I didn't know how to put all those skills together. I needed to listen to how people talked, learn how they thought, even learn the slang of regular people. I was rooted in the classics, trained in archaic languages and esoteric survival skills. I had never read magazines or hung out with people. As I thought my proficiency with copywriting improved, Bob became increasingly alarmed.

One night he asked me, "You have no idea what normal people need or want, do you?"

I had never thought of that as a deficiency.

"To be a copywriter you have to hit people's hot buttons. You need to know what motivates them, what their everyday dreams are about."

I had no idea what normal people thought about.

DRAGONS LOOK UP

The plains of Bagan, Myanmar · They say there are special places on this planet. I have been to many: Ayers Rock, the Black Hills, Tibet, Angkor Wat, and others. One of the most memorable is an Asian place of seething insurgencies, where a group of generals is ruled by a man who worships the number nine. I call Wink in Thailand and tell him to meet me in Yangon in two days.

The plains of Bagan in Myanmar are a mystical place even for those who don't believe. In the daylight this army of temples and monuments is a spectacle that has impressed for thousands of years, exotic, massive, and crouched. Each structure is unique, painstaking in its construction. This is not a dangerous place but I have chosen to make it dangerous. I am here to meet with the banned political party of Aung San Suu Kyi. "Unsung Sushi" we call her, the wife of an intellectual, daughter of a famous liberator, symbol of resistance. She has fared poorly in this land of generals.

The phone in the hotel is tapped. When we call the secret number, I can hear someone patch in. Sometimes people will tell us not to call this number, it is too risky. Finally we are told to make a secret rendezvous. Someone will take us to the person we want to meet. "Make sure you are not followed."

After the meeting, the secret police follow me and ask obvious questions about which people we talked to. They check with the hotel clerk, asking where we have been. Our guide is a former military officer who has badly translated his business cards to read "Lonely Tours." He thinks using the name of a popular travel guide will increase his business. He always carries a fat book with pictures of happy customers. He says he can take us to the fighting in the west. But with the heat on me I just want to see the sights: the golden temples of Shwedayon, the massive stupas in the country, a land not yet discovered by the hordes.

I am delaying my return as I always do. There is something to be learned here but I do not know what.

In Bagan, a village that has been bulldozed to make it more seemly for tourists, we ride the river. Over there, on that riverbank, a foreigner disappeared. Can we help find him? Probably not.

Over there is a great annual festival that coincides with the full moon. Yes, that is what I want.

That night Wink and I climb the temples. I am in a petrified forest of swooping, star-bound spaceships. The cold colorless light of the moon outlines a world unlike any I have ever seen. Far below, people walk, crunching in the dry sand.

I do not want to go back. I am happy running, at high speed, through danger, past even the most remote and unseen places. There is something here that's deeper than religion, a timeless window to what makes life worth living.

The moon winks at me from behind a gracefully hung stupa. The sense of ages laughs at me. You see the answer before you.

This is what you must do.

THE WORDS BELOW
THE PICTURES

Toronto, Ontario · Although I moved from the mail room to the creative department, I was not handed the agency's top account. I occupied my time writing things like truck catalogs and baby food ads from a small booth where the audiovisual equipment was kept. I did double duty as the AV geek racking up commercials, taping focus groups, and making dubs. I also worked on a few song and dance shows, helped on some award-winning ads, did game shows, and spent a lot of time learning just what this advertising thing was. At night I spent long hours with Bob discussing life and advertising. Back in Victoria my friends were still in their first year of college and beginning to plan for their big trip to Europe in the spring.

Despite my original passion, my work was oddly unsatisfying. I found writing ridiculous things about dull products that serve only to catch the eye for a few seconds and then disappear forever silly. Some of the writers would critique my writing, warning me that you couldn't call a powerful new delivery truck a "snub-nosed mother." They liked words like "delicious," "satisfying," and even "chocolaty." BBDO was famous for being a dull agency that toiled for long-term clients like Kodak and Carnation. Nobody rocked the boat, everyone rowed. So I toiled and learned. In one of my many late-night talks with Bob I told him of my frustration. He sympathized. He told me that he had started working when he was nineteen, gotten married, bought a house, and had kids. Now here he was at fifty at the top of his game and he had never done anything he really wanted to do. He told me that he had dreamed of travel and adventure and just wandering, being a free spirit. I was shocked. I assumed that to be famous, wealthy, and respected was all you needed in this life, that a man at the top of his career, with an expensive house full of kids, a wife he had been with for decades, and a sense of what was right, should not be talking about being a failure.

Cautiously I mentioned that my high school friends wanted me to go to Europe with them but that I didn't want to ruin my chances of becoming a full-fledged copywriter. Bob suggested that maybe I should think about taking a leave of absence, something usually accorded to senior executives who have drinking problems or are going back to school. He encouraged me to travel, see the world, learn about life and learn about people. He told me that I was too intense for this job, fought too hard for ideas, refused to be mundane. He said that if I continued I would end up burned-out and disillusioned in a few years and that I could always come back and pick up where I left off.

Flabbergasted that I would be offered a leave of absence, I pondered the idea. I was a seventeen-year-old copywriter with no road map for the future. I didn't realize that in just over one year I had achieved one of my lifelong dreams and run out of map.

I decided to go to Europe. I saved my money, bought a ticket on the SS *Canberra* for $120, and got my bike ready to bicycle across Europe. When I ran out of money, I would come back. After all, how long could it take to see the world?

MEN WITHOUT WOMEN

Guatemala City, Guatemala · I traveled out of a tiny red Karrimor backpack. I had bought the pack in England three years ago before I went to Europe for the first time. The small backpack was comforting, like an old friend. I was looking for a tropical island so I could do nothing. I took the train, buses, hitchhiked, and hung out.

When things were slow, I would write in my diary. But there are only so many times you can write about writing in your diary. In Guatemala I went to buy an English-language book. It had to be small to fit in my pack. The smallest one I could find was a collection of short stories called *Men Without Women*, by Ernest Hemingway.

I had never truly read the archaic, pretentious prose of Hemingway. I had always thought Hemingway was a man who created a fictional world to hide his real one. But the book was cheap and small. It made the nights pass quickly.

I liked to reread certain stories. I would order a strong coffee in my hotel in Guatemala and sit outside listening to the gunfire that rang out throughout the night. I would smoke cigarettes and reread the shortest stories until I thought I knew what Hemingway was trying to say. He would write around what was happening, forcing readers to fill in the blanks with their own emotions and experiences. My favorite story was "Hills Like White Elephants." I liked the lack of direct focus, the sense of emotional numbness hiding deep hurt. I didn't know it was a fabrication. Surely reality must be the "only true thing," as Hemingway liked to call it.

As I traveled through each country in Central America, I came face-to-face with warfare, devastation, poverty, injustice, and its people. I started to look at the world through a writer's eyes. I also started to write down the simple things I did. I learned Spanish from menus, asked people to draw me maps of where I was going. I had no idea that I was traveling through dangerous places. I was focused on the people around me, not the politics. The odd Westerner would warn me to be careful. Even the rebels, when they stopped the buses at gunpoint, would want to know why I was here. I asked them why they were here. Despite the danger, things made sense, people connected, I learned the hard way, the right way.

I kept reading Hemingway. When I neared Panama, I realized I could begin filling in the blank spaces, but like an artist with missing colors, I felt I was missing something.

THE ISLAND

San Andrés Island, Colombia · I had always wanted to live on a tropical island but I had never seen one, let alone been to one. My life had been in the hard north. I found an island on a map, the most remote one I could find. San Andrés was just off the coast of Nicaragua. It was a short flight from Panama to the Colombian-owned speck. I had no idea that San Andrés was famed for drug running, uninhibited Colombian girls on vacation, corrupt officials, wholesale smuggling, and even pirates. I was to find even more.

I first saw Jean while drinking a free drink with Shawn and Richard. Richard was a six-foot-six burly ex–Coast Guard swabbie in town to get his friend out of jail. When he saw another gringo on the tiny Caribbean island, he demanded that I stop walking wherever I was going and have a drink on him. I was "Buddy" to him and he kept me as a drunken hostage that day.

A tall blonde woman walked up and asked in a matronly manner whether Richard had heard from the lawyer. Jean had long hair, a lithe figure, and a shy, gentle demeanor. I was spellbound when I saw her green eyes. She would later tell me that when she first saw me I looked into her soul and it frightened her. I was told she was there to get two people out of jail as well. We were introduced and said goodbye.

The next day I saw Richard on the beach, chain-smoking cigarettes. Jean was there in a lime-green bikini. She asked about my peeling back. Spending hours and days on the reef had turned me a dark brown but I continued to peel. After putting hot coconut oil on my shoulders and back she began to rub and massage my back in a way that told me she wanted me to know something. I didn't know what to do or say, I just knew that something was happening.

Jean was twenty-nine years old, married to a newscaster but separated and living with her eleven-year-old daughter. I was nineteen. She was friends with Ray Jay, a drug dealer in Norman, Oklahoma. Ray Jay had hired unsuspecting college girls to come to Colombia to ferry back drugs. They would get a couple of thousand dollars to carry cocaine wrapped in condoms stuffed in their vaginas. Pregnant women worked best. Ray was smart for this game but on this run he had screwed up on the mainland and when he had arrived in San Andrés he had been busted. His pregnant accomplice had been searched and they were in deep shit.

The women's jail was a simple house with no fence, no walls, and no locks on the door. I went with Jean to visit her friends and the news looked good: her friends might go free for a price. A local lawyer would arrange the appropriate discussions and payoffs. During the time I spent with Jean I found more than adventure, however; I found love. I had never known women before and Jean was more than I expected. She considered me wise, funny, and stable. I found her warm, caring, and passionate. When the time came for her to secretly leave the island with her friends, I became more aware of my feelings. The thought of her slipping into the night and never seeing me again ripped a large hole in me.

I made my feelings known but she didn't know what to do. She slipped a ring with two bells on my finger and said, "Deliver this to me in Oklahoma."

WILDFIRE

Norman, Oklahoma · I had traveled as far as money and interest could take me. I could continue as a beach bum on San Andrés or I could start another journey.

I looked down at the silver ring Jean had given me. It symbolized something and consumed me. Why would she give me this ring and tell me to bring it to her in Oklahoma? There was a strong emotional pull but I knew that there was no happy ending. I flew to Miami and bummed a ride with a couple taking a drive-away Pinto to Seattle. I slept in the car, survived on beer and peanut butter sandwiches, and took turns flipping the buttons on the AM radio as we drove the hot, flat miles to Oklahoma.

Along the way I tried to call Jean but every time I called, her phone was busy or would ring and ring. I had a feeling of dread. What if this wasn't her phone number, what if she didn't even live in Norman? When I was within fifty miles, I was excited. Jean's phone was still busy. I kept reading the small piece of paper with the address she had given me.

When I arrived at the small apartment, my heart was in my mouth. I rang the doorbell, no one was home. I jimmied a window and then dropped my red pack inside. It was then I heard a man's voice. She was with someone. Embarrassed, I abandoned my pack inside her house and went to a nearby shopping mall. All the men looked like football players, all the girlfriends like cheerleaders. It seemed like everyone drove black Firebirds or Camaros. Tired of walking around, I went back to Jean's apartment.

She was thrilled to see me. "Oh God, you came back to me" was how she greeted me. Now I was getting confused. She made me lunch, then said, "Come with me to the bedroom. I want to be made love to."

A heavy chain around my heart snapped.

We had a couple of days together and spent much of it talking.

Jean's story was that her husband was the first man she had ever slept with. She was the perfect loving wife until something went wrong. She wouldn't tell me what it was but they were working on a divorce. Jean starting going to university and dating. She discovered a world she never knew existed, one that triggered emotions and passions she had never known. Then she met me, someone who had the uncanny ability to not only read her mind but tell her what she was thinking and who she was.

One day while we were lying in bed the phone rang. It was Jean's husband and somehow he knew she was with someone. There was a lot of crying and anger and she hung up the phone. It would be best if I stayed with Dianne, the pregnant friend we had helped get out of jail in San Andrés. My emotions started to go out of control. To come this far, be this happy, and then have it all dashed was too much, too soon.

Dianne's world was a very different place. She and her bearded, longhaired husband lived in a communal house. I never did figure out who else lived there. Old, young, criminal, straight, gay, came and went. Their only common bond was sex and drugs, usually from people making transcon drug runs. All that was required to crash day or night was a sample tossed on the coffee table in the living room. There was always a wrinkled foil brick, Baggie, or conical stack of white powder for all to sample. And there was always a party going on. Heroin, mushrooms, cocaine, hash, LSD, grass, it was a psychedelic buffet for anyone that walked in.

Finally, in a moment of clarity, I went to see Jean. She was touched by my devotion but it was over. Not emotionally but in practicality.

Like awaking from a dream, I packed my small red bag, bummed a ride to Highway 40, and hitchhiked to Victoria.

THE MENTORED

Toronto, Ontario · Eventually I made it back to Toronto and became a copywriter again. Things were very different. I returned to BBDO to find that Bob McAlear was dead. Apparently, shortly after I had gone to Europe, Bob left his wife and eight kids, moved to the south of Spain, bought a monkey, and had his ear pierced. He spent his days reading poetry, sipping wine, and talking with the locals, just living and learning, I guess.

He was gone for about six months. Then he came back, got back with his wife, took out the earring, had a heart attack, and died. At the funeral everyone agreed—he had died happy.

THE LOOK

Toronto, Ontario, December 9, 1975 · I first saw my wife when I visited my high school friend at his co-op apartment in Toronto. I was twenty, had been around the world and had a number of jobs, but my friends were still in university. Students lived together in run-down brick homes and shared chores to save money. Linda and John took the garbage out. They had become friends, then lovers.

When I first saw her, she was wearing overalls and seemed a little silly. When she first saw me, I was wearing a snap-down cowboy shirt, shooting glasses, yellow boots, and an expensive Aquascutum raincoat. My normal daytime garb was a three-piece suit, but my only casual clothes came from my days as a driller and a lumberjack. Just like my personality, I didn't see any dividing line between the two. John, Linda, and I ended up as an odd threesome when we went to movies or to bars. I didn't dislike her, I just thought she came from another planet. John, the son of upper-middle-class suburban parents, was a raving Marxist and into odd European cars like Tatras and Citroëns. Linda was about as mainstream as you could get, industrious, socially chatty, eternally cheerful. She had English parents who lived in the same house, went home every Sunday for dinner, and was training to be a schoolteacher.

When John moved back to Victoria for the summer, Linda and I would spend the days hanging around and having fun. It was refreshing to have my ideas and lifestyle tested by someone who was different from me in every physical and mental way.

Then one day we realized we had fallen in love. It was a slow, solid love. Not a wildfire, more like the slow-burning embers of an oak fire. When she told me she was moving to England to live, I cried. She stayed. We lived together and then married.

IN SEARCH OF PIRATES

Semporna, Sabah · I am intrigued by the idea of modern-day pirates who prey on fishermen and cargo ships, pulling alongside in their speedboats and then overpowering or killing their victims. The hub of this activity is the shallow archipelago that connects the south of the Philippines with the northeast of Borneo. Here, hundreds of small islands and villages built in the coral shallows hide smugglers and pirates.

Semporna is not much of a town, rows of grim, two-story, cement buildings with goods spilling into the streets from the stores below. It is a trading town that acts as a magnet for gypsies, smugglers, and fighters. The Moros also live here, Muslims who have been fighting a war in the nearby southern Philippines. It is a center for fishing and sea produce: pearls, seaweed farms. It is also a diving center, with Sipadan as the main attraction. Since I am starting to look as if I belong in the jungle, I decide to treat myself to a hotel. I choose the Dragon Inn because it is built over the water.

I am also looking forward to a good meal. The Dragon Inn is famous for its fresh seafood. I am learning that the Chinese love to look at animals before they eat them. The sharks, tuna, crabs, lobster, and fish on display in the inn's aquarium are also on the menu. It is quite acceptable to have your picture taken with your meal while it is still alive.

Dinner is both deep and shallow water lobster, grouper, fried rice, and hot-and-sour soup. Sitting over the water, I watch the sun go down in a tropical sunset that fades through blues, purples, golds, yellows, and then bloodred, before revealing a canopy of brilliant stars against a deep blue sky.

Later I wander around the town. The pool halls are bustling, and I hear the quiet chatter of people having dinner. I go to sleep to the sound of lapping waves, interrupted by the sound of rats scurrying and scraping along the roof and inside the walls.

Morning is announced by the sound of outboard motors, and the cool green light of the water coming between the gaps in the hardwood floors. I bathe out back using water scooped out of a large ceramic jar. The toilet seems to go into a pipe, but since I have yet to see a functioning sewer system, it probably dumps straight into the crystal-clear water. The multipurpose function of the ocean as provider and receptor is dubious when I consider that the dinner I had last night came out of the same ocean about fifty feet away.

My favorite time of the day is dawn. In Africa morning breaks like the sharp click of a shell being ejected from a carbine. In Borneo morning rises softly out of the sea. It is a glorious day. The call to prayer is played over and over as if to wake those who overslept. The evening's monsoon showers have cleansed the streets of last night's garbage and freshened the air, the sun bathing everything in a honey-eyed light reflected from the gold-painted domes of the mosque and beckoning me to the market.

The bustling marketplace of Semporna is built over the water and is a good introduction to the smells, sounds, and colors of this part of Sabah. Indonesians, Filipinos, Bajaus, Malays, Chinese, Indians, and Arabs mingle in this Asian kaleidoscope. I wander among clouds of frying grease and the smells of enticing spices, animals, and exotic vegetables. Long silver fish grin back at me as they sit stacked in neat rows. I see barracuda, salted and split into ornate shapes; sharks, whose fins have been removed and sold to restaurants; *siri* leaves, a type of pepper used with betel nut; *tarap*, a yellow breadfruit with spiky flesh, found only in Borneo. There are giant jackfruits *(nangka)*, star fruit, coffee grinders, ice shavers, and sago (brightly colored starch made into drinks). The rats slither like harried commuters between the crates and refuse while pus-ridden cats stare groggily at passersby.

Old ladies perch on counters with the classic market pose—one leg under, one leg up, supporting a hand on the forehead. Their eyes flicker, waiting for the ever-so-slight hesitation that means someone may be interested. Sensing a customer, they click into their animated spiel: "We have the finest produce, there is no better price." Once they see you are just browsing, they revert to the pose. Prices are so low it is not even worth haggling, but it must be done. The next *orang puti*, or white man, will always pay what the most gullible has paid before. The Sea Bajaus, the Gypsies of the Sea, bring their dried fish and cucumbers here to exchange. The pirates meet here to exchange information and arrange smuggling contracts. But who is a gypsy and who is a pirate? Here, the line is blurred.

After the close, fetid smell of the market, the brilliant pure light of the ocean with its exotic silhouettes beckons. On the dock the slimy tidal muck is visible through the worn rounded planks. Care must be taken if you step toward the ends of these rotted boards, since great economy is taken with the use of nails.

That afternoon I arrange for a speedboat to take me out to meet the Sea Bajaus. They can be found in Sabah as far as Papar, particularly in the area of the Tempasuk Plain, and on the west coast of Sabah, concentrated around Semporna.

The Bajaus are Filipino by descent. Today they are fishermen, farmers, trappers of crabs, collectors of sea cucumbers and shellfish. Some also cut firewood in mangrove swamps. Their nomadic life dictates that their profession be waterborne. On the west coast of Sabah, Sea Bajaus are traditionally farmers; some grow rice, others raise cattle, bison, or ponies. The Spanish introduced horses to the Philippines, and the Bajaus brought the horses with them. Because of their skill with horses, the Bajau horsemen are known as the Cowboys of Asia.

The Sea Bajaus who choose to live in villages build their homes over the tidal flats of Semporna. At first it is disconcerting to see a rustic thatched village standing completely on its own and out of sight of any terra firma. On closer inspection there are two reasons why these villages make sense. First, the water is a shallow three to six feet deep for miles around. Second, being on the edge of the flats lets the fishermen build their homes on stilts directly over their fishing and crabbing grounds.

The Sea Bajaus who live on boats have a simpler, more elegant existence. Their *lipa-lipa* are beautifully carved, some with intricately carved bows and latticework windows. They have all the comforts of home: stove, sleeping areas, cages for animals. Many even drag their in-laws behind them in a separate boat. Typically there is a main boat that tows small canoes behind it, sometimes as many as three.

Out to sea, I see a line of boats like elephants on parade. My boatman, Ahmed, revs the engine to catch up. Like Arab traders, this flotilla is a self-sufficient community. Their hand-carved wooden boats are faded to a light gray. Fish hang from sticks that protrude from the boats. Small fish are laid out to dry on thatched roofs. On one roof is a barracuda, slit and splayed in a delicate zigzag pattern. Chickens are kept in woven or wooden lattice cages. Laundry, tools, and supplies hang in careful arrangements. Towed behind, a small girl is cleaning giant clams in a tiny canoe. The look is very much Depression-era Okie, with elegantly carved boats replacing clattering pickup trucks. Their poverty is extreme, even by Asian standards, but it is apparent that these are happy people. It could be argued that because they depend on the sea and want for nothing, they, like most nomads, are rich.

At dusk we head back to the Dragon Inn for another multicourse seafood dinner. On the way back the outboard motor conks out. Ahmed busies himself sucking gas, cleaning plugs, and swapping engines every ten minutes until we slide into the dock. I clean up the debris in the boat and pack it into a plastic bag. As I climb the ten feet up to the dock, Ahmed takes the carefully packed trash and empty film canisters and tosses them into the ocean.

The next day I decide to put a little edge on the trip and head out into the shipping lanes and small islands to search for pirates. As I lose sight of land, the feeling that there is danger here increases. These are pirate waters. Not just the armed paramilitary that robs freighters, but vicious Indonesians and Filipino pirates that prey on gentle fishermen. Just one week ago a gang of five pirates used M-16s to rob a local fisherman of his motor and a battery. There are weekly reports of fishing boats being stolen and people being killed, robbed, and raped for their meager possessions. Banks are robbed in coastal towns, entire cargo ships are relieved of their safes, and sailors of their valuables. My load of expensive cameras and other gear would definitely interest them. Our outboards are cantankerous, and I am without food, water, or emergency equipment. I probably qualify as stupid, rather than as adventurous.

I had asked Ahmed to bring snorkels, ice, and lunches, and of course, after swearing up and down that it would be no problem, he brought nothing. I silently decide who will be eaten first, should we be set adrift: Ahmed.

As we head for open ocean, we pass a group of fishermen leaving their small island. The small border post flies the Malaysian flag, so I know we are getting close to Indonesia. The fishermen have set out in a collection of dugout canoes, motorboats, pirogues, and outriggers to perform a questionable act: fishing by bomb. Using fertilizer as a base, they concoct a mixture that creates a massive explosion that ruptures the internal flotation organs of the reef fish. Then they dive into the water to pick up the stunned and dead fish. You can tell if your fish has been caught by bombing because its insides are destroyed. No one has calculated how much damage has been done to the coral reefs by this crude method of fishing, but it continues every day.

We pass a number of light gray houses built over the water. These are crabbing villages. The villagers drop their crab-catching baskets from their front doors and the waste from the village feeds the crabs. A simple but questionable exchange of resources. I visit, take pictures, talk with the people. No pirates here.

Among the hundreds of tiny islands we find a tiny spot of sand that is the best example of the mythical desert island I have ever seen, Pulau Umusan. One lonely coconut palm, a handful of grass shacks, the rusting hulk of a wrecked boat, and twenty people who make their living collecting and drying sea cucumbers. The majority of them are Obian Filipino and Sulu. The women fastidiously arrange the sea cucumbers they gather to dry, turning them religiously. The children play in the water as if on vacation. We stop and marvel at the adaptability of people.

The rain hisses on the water as we make our way back. We pass the stilt villages we visited earlier: Gagangun, Pulau Tiga, Pulau Putih. Off in the distance is the silhouette of the ever-present police boat.

The sun comes out. The tin-covered mosque domes glow golden against the dark green coco palms. The twisted, rickety stilt villages are now shimmering silhouettes dwarfed by pure white tropical thunderheads in the dark blue sky. They could be mirages. My thoughts of pirates gone, we head peacefully into the dock at Semporna. As I clean up my belongings, this time making sure I take my film boxes and refuse with me, one of the longhaired men at the dock looks down into the boat and notices the empty SX-70 Polaroid film battery packs. He yells to my boatman in a regional dialect that sounds like Tagalog. Ahmed asks me in a curiously serious and polite tone, "Do you have need of these?" as he holds the flat batteries up.

I reply, not quite understanding Ahmed's sudden eco-correctness, "No, but they should be disposed of properly because they are caustic."

"My friend would like them," Ahmed replies with a shit-eating grin.

I look up to his Ray Banned friend, complete with a dangling Marlboro, and then back at Ahmed. He gives me his best "hello to my tourist friend" smile back.

"Why does he want them?" I inquire.

"They are worth a lot of money."

While I am wracking my brain for what possible use a boatman and his dubious, deeply tanned associate would have for used batteries, Ahmed finally comes clean.

"We need them for our bomb timers."

I have found my pirates.

THE SUMMIT

Torrance, California · My wife and I had a working marriage. She was the rock and I was the balloon; this was important since I needed that stability and predictability and she liked the nonstop energy. I had stuck to the grindstone in Toronto, worked as a tunneler and blaster's assistant in between my job at BBDO, managed a hardware store, and then, feeling underemployed, seized on the opportunity to do a multimedia show about Toronto for tourists. I spent two years on the

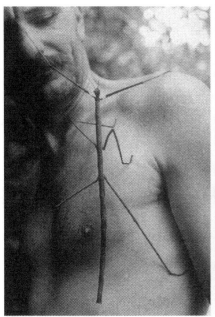

The stick insect is the world's largest and gentlest insect.

It finds my face to be an excellent resting spot.

A break in the action.

*Traveling along the
Niger River in Mali.*

The ultimate test of waterproof boots.

*Writing becomes a necessary
part of every journey I take.*

When it rains in Borneo, you wash.

After an evening of drinking in a Sarawak longhouse.

He's Bad. He's Windy. He's a TOURIST WITH AN ATTITUDE

The first indication that what I do might be of interest to others was an Outside *magazine profile.*

A charming old lady in East Turkey. She lives in a cave that will soon be underwater.

I have a talent for rolling Land Rovers. Luckily, you just winch them back up and keep going.

Here's a shot from a recent CNN appearance. Somehow I became a pundit on dangerous places. I didn't realize how few journalists actually go there to gather news firsthand.

My greatest adventure and greatest achievement. Lisa and Claire at age sixteen.

Visiting with captured Talib prisoners of war in Northern Afghanistan.

RYP, Coskun Aral, Ali Bucak, and bodyguards in Severik, Turkey.

A shy rebel group called the RPA ABB decided to let me be the first to film them. During the process, I suggested getting a snappier name and losing the earmuffs.

Shooting a travel show in Afghanistan is like shooting an X-rated film in a convent. You can do it, but no one will believe it's true.

Rebel leaders seem to appreciate that I just want to find out how people live, not get into the political morass.

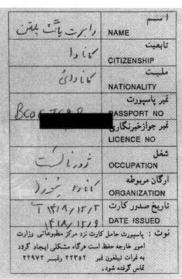

شماره کارت

اسم
NAME
رابرت یاش پلتن

تابعیت
CITIZENSHIP
کانادا

ملیت
NATIONALITY
کانادای

نمبر پاسپورت
PASSPORT NO
Bco●●●●●●

نمبر جواز خبرنگاری
LICENCE NO

شغل
OCCUPATION
ژورنالست

ارگان مربوطه
ORGANIZATION
کانادا شیرزد

تاریخ صدور کارت
DATE ISSUED
۱۴۱۸/۱۲/۳
۱۴۱۸/۱۲/۲۹

مرکز مطبوعاتی وزارت امور خارجه دولت اسلامی افغانستان باکمال احترام از تمام مقامات دولتی وامنیتی کشور آرزومند است تابا حامل کارت از هیچگونه همکاری ممکن دریغ نورزند.

نوت : پاسپورت حامل کارت نزد مرکز مطبوعاتی وزارت امور خارجه حفظ است مرگ، مشکلی ایجاد گردد به نمرات تیلفون نمبر ۲۲۳۵۲ دفتر ۲۲۹۷۲ تماس گرفته شود.

رئیس مرکز مطبوعاتی
وزارت امور خارجه

Yes, you do need a visa to visit the rebels.

A happy passport picture just makes you look like an idiot when you get killed.

streets of Toronto interviewing people, taking photographs, and writing the script. I wasn't supposed to—I was supposed to be the liaison between the American producer and the writer—but I became absorbed. The result was an hour-long sixty-four-projected, 16mm film, complete with special effects, and it ran for years. People laughed, they cried, they applauded, they came back. I used the experience, awards, and notoriety I gained from producing the show to get a special visa to move to the States. I had been to the States before and hadn't liked the brash, tacky ambience. But one time I went to Los Angeles, went for a walk on the beach at sunset, and for some reason suddenly felt like I was home.

Linda was not thrilled about leaving Toronto and the comfortable cocoon of her life, but she did. When we moved to California, we added up our net worth. A rusted Honda Accord and a bill for $2,000 from the movers. A negative net worth.

We took a small oceanfront apartment in the South Bay and I made the commute to the Hollywood cesspool to create multimedia shows. I was a designer, created the look and pace of launches for products like the Macintosh, motorcycles, university fund-raisers, car stereos, and whatever. The job was high-stress and I took it in by the ton. Working all night was typical, creating, coordinating, and laying out thousands of elements. On the drive home at night I would zone out and would only find my freeway exit by hitting a certain pothole before the exit.

Nevertheless it was an idyllic period, because when I did get home I would change into my bathing suit and walk out the door. The ocean would erase any concerns I had. Linda and I were having a honeymoon we never had.

I knew when we conceived children. It is a special feeling unique to love and marriage. Linda stayed at home and grew in size while I figured out how to make a living. We had identical twin daughters. I took pictures of the girls being sliced out of their mother's stomach and then rushed home to buy a crib.

Just before the girls were born I took stock of my situation. I had no job, no savings, so I decided to buy a house on borrowed money and start a business. As usual everything worked out fine. I spent my days renovating the simple 1955 house and looking after the twins. I worked out of a spare bedroom in the house and did bigger work in the garage. I would stuff one girl apiece into the pockets on either side of my bathrobe and write business plans. The girls would stare up at me as I typed proposals and wrote pitch letters. I was all I wanted to be, providing warmth, energy, and love to these tiny humans.

My efforts paid off. Business came in. I had no backer, no staff, not even a business phone, so I improvised. I rented a ten-thousand-square-foot office on the beach in Hermosa. I began to have a staff, to travel, wear suits, go to meetings, prepare budgets. I was in business.

Since I was a one-man band, I also had to stage the shows I produced in Miami, Acapulco, Torremolinos, Monte Carlo, Berlin, and other cities. Employees who were in sales or even answered the phone became staging crews. I made it work and I made money doing good work.

My wife was not pleased that I was away from home so much and that I worked so late and so long. But like a sailor in a squall, I just ignored the threats and did what I had to do.

AFRICA

Toronto, Ontario · It's hard to describe a continent, and Africa is divided into dissimilar parts. There is the Horn, a heat-blasted hell of dried animal carcasses and bucktoothed *mooryans*, the land of blood feuds and heartless thievery. There is the *mahgreb*, the western world of Islam, a dry, hot, mountainous land with a Mediterranean rim, a safe place except for Algeria, where a government wars on its own people. The shores of North Africa are a rich, indolent place where people once fed and inebriated the entire Roman Empire with their wheat and grapes, a land of empty ruins, great hospitality, and sparse elegance.

There is the West, a land of color, cultural clashes, and forced stability, albeit a criminal or colonial one. This area is only embarrassed by the two nations set up as free homelands for the slaves, one American, one British, both disasters. Liberia and Sierra Leone have no future, no hope, only the constant nihilistic friction of dissonant cultures.

There is the South. A land of safaris, superficial civilization, careening economies, and Western influence. A land unraveling in chaos on its east and west extremities as well as in its center.

There are the Great Lakes, the countries that border the Great Rift Valley, the cradle of man and the wellspring of the Apocalypse. Here colonial influence still flutters, ripped and bloodstained in the wind. A land where there has been a great war between the Nilotics and Bantus but no one dares to intervene. A place so devolved that there is no law, no hope, no money, no future. Only warfare and survival. This is an abandoned world of mildewed, looted architecture and kids with bloodshot eyes wielding AKs with the stocks sawed off.

For years I had carefully taped, untaped, and retaped the three Michelin maps that make up the entire continent of Africa on my walls. This giant map of Africa formed a six-foot idol that always sat facing my bed in my bachelor life. When I began married life, I carefully untaped and refolded each map, taking great pains to not lose the hours of visual adventure they contained.

When I talked to people about my fascination with the "dark continent," I was warned off by everyone I consulted. First my doctor went over a long list of incurable tropic parasites that awaited me: snail-borne parasites that burrow through your skin to stay lodged in your large intestine for life; insects that lay parasitic eggs inside your body that emerge from a blister in your leg (when you can't stand it anymore you can pull out the three-foot-long worm, but only a bit at a time using a small stick to twist the worm around); worms that live inside your eyeball until you mercifully go blind; maggots that grow under your skin and eat your flesh; spinal meningitis that comes from the wind off the Sahara; strange diseases from monkey bites; quinine-resistant malaria from tiny mosquitoes. How much did I want to hear before I gave up my crazy idea? My travel agent would talk about plane crashes and hijacking. Fellow travelers all had tales of horror, and newspapers were full of stories about war, famine, revolution, and slaughter.

Still, despite my new life as a businessman, creative dynamo, and family man, something was tugging at me. Someday I would go to Africa.

JET SET

Monte Carlo, Monaco · MAI Basic Four was a computer company that soon became my biggest client. Being an international company meant that exotic places like Hawaii were too mundane and far away for their sales meetings, so Monaco was chosen as the next site. I was hired to put together a program and a show and worked to polish every detail. Although the U.S. employees thought Cary Grant and Grace Kelly still strolled the streets of Monaco, the Europeans called it Las Vegas Plage in reference to the crass commercialization, glitz, and high prices. I could see why.

In between taking photos for the show, I would walk down to the harbor. Monte Carlo is home to the most conspicuous icon of wealth, the yacht. Sitting side by side in the harbor, mere 150-foot yachts were dwarfed by 250-foot yachts, complete with crews, matching tenders, and designer-label uniforms. On deck owners sat in their white bathrobes drinking mimosas and wondering what would get them through their day. My favorite image was of a diffident, monogrammed and bathrobed yacht owner posing for an assembled crowd of gawkers, standing below the stern of his boat. The object of the crowd's interest? Not the matching napkins on the table, but the owner's testicles swinging below his short bathrobe. Such are the simple pleasures of the poor.

The show went off flawlessly despite the habit of the French technicians to never show up and when they did, leave with our equipment stuffed in their pockets. Creating, writing, producing, and staging complex, high-stress shows was becoming routine for me. The bigger the better, the more stress the more I liked it.

After our show was over, the crew and I went hunting for some late-night entertainment, ending up at Jimmy Z's. To experience the spectacle of Jimmy Z's on an off-night, not only had we had to stand in line for hours but we'd also had to convince the door wench that we were the only genetic alternative to inbreeding that night.

At about 5:00 A.M., tired of the bacchanalian event, I returned to my hotel feeling very unsettled. I was thirty, a millionaire, drove a Rolls-Royce, had a nice house, a loving wife, two perfect children, a successful business, perfect health, and a future ahead of me. So what was bugging me?

THE CALL

Monte Carlo, Monaco · I couldn't sleep, so I went up to the cement terrace of the hotel to watch the sun rise. The Mediterranean was smooth with small ridges coming toward me from the south. A light wind brought a smell to me I could not recognize but entranced me. It was earthy, rich, fecund, and spiced. It was Africa. I had forgotten that across this dull gray pond and hours away from this fantasyland of excess lay a land of my dreams.

I watched the bowl of the horizon shift through the spectrum of dawn, and by the time the sun glanced across the water I had made up my mind. I could smell Africa and it was calling me.

That morning I called Linda and explained that I had to go to Africa. She wasn't pleased but she didn't have much choice.

I bought a ticket to Bamako, the capital of Mali. My goal was to meet the Dogon people and from that point who knew? It was the hottest month of the year in the Sahara. Temperatures in the shade would average around 140 degrees. The hotel barber refused to shave my head. "I am a barber, not a butcher, monsieur!" We agreed on a modified version of the legion *boule* cut. I looked like an escapee from a mental home but I was smiling when it was done.

THE SPECTER

Somewhere in French Sahara · I know I am getting sicker. I am reduced to spending hours lying on the grubby, thin mattress. When it gets soaked with my sweat, I roll onto the dusty concrete floor in search of coolness. Puddles of sweat crawl slowly out of me like blood from a sniper victim. I am too weak to get up. Too tired to eat. Too stupefied by fever to think straight. I pull myself to the corner with the stinking drain as fluids pour out of my shivering body. I don't know how many star-filled nights I have lain on this concrete floor. I can see the stars through the open metal door. I can actually see them move, like a video being played in slow motion. Time has been disconnected.

Deep into the night in the deadly, godless silence of the Sahara I think I hear two men approaching. They shuffle slowly, banging the metal doors as they search the rooms of the empty *campement.* I can hear them coming closer but I can't move. In the blackness of my cell I can't tell if I am awake or dreaming. A few days earlier a man had jumped through my window and been surprised to find me in the room. He fled in terror. Is he back for my life or my money?

The steps are getting closer. Too weak to move, I lie in the dark of the moonless night and await my fate. Finally the steps are at my door. I try to make out a shape or form in the darkness. The door clangs open and reveals a silhouette. Looking up, I see my nemesis: an inquisitive donkey.

Death did not come for me but he introduced himself.

THE KNOCK

Irvine, California · In California my business was growing rapidly. My mentor, protector, and client during my work for MAI Basic Four was Bob Mobilia. A bullnecked, spring-wound man with a balding bullet head, he took everything he did seriously.

There was no confusion as to where I stood with Bob. When I screwed up, I took the full brunt of his displeasure and then I got down to fixing it. Bob worked for an even tougher taskmaster, Bill Patton. Bill Patton's taskmaster was Ben LeBow, a well-known corporate raider and wheeler-dealer. It seemed most of his ventures were companies stuck in first gear that seemed to sprint ahead on paper but in reality were stretched to the limits to meet growth and debt demands. We had been working a financial presentation to make MBF an attractive acquisition for another large computer company. Suddenly I was given the job of making MBF look like an attractive *acquirer* of a computer company.

The company they set their sights on was Prime Computer, a

billion-dollar company that MBF had approached as a seller and been rudely rebuffed. The gist of the story was that LeBow then decided that he was going to show them by leading a hostile takeover.

It didn't work and after the lawyers pocketed around $25 million in fees MBF was an empty, hollow shell.

The ax had swung and executives filed out with their possessions in quickly folded banker's boxes. Bob stayed and we soldiered on.

One day Bob had a sling on his arm. He had been playing racquetball and broken his collarbone. The next month it was not healing. His body was riddled with bone cancer. I visited Bob as he turned from a robust fireplug of a man into a skeleton. He lay in bed, his breath coming in thin gulps and his skin pulled tightly over his skull. The effects of the painkillers dulled his mind and although I would sit and talk to him, the Bob I knew had already died. The last time I saw him I kissed him gently on the forehead and said good-bye. A rope slipped into the water and I was cast adrift again.

HE WHO NEVER KNEW

Calgary, Alberta · My father was living in Calgary. The company he had worked for most of his life was his main focus. He sold industrial equipment to large construction projects and his job was to get in on the bidding process early, spec the right equipment, and make sure he got the job. My father didn't engage in anything other than doing the best job, gaining the trust of engineers, and making sure every detail was taken care of. The two owners of the company promised him large stock options, gave him plenty of freedom to fly his plane, and never really looked over his shoulder. My father loved to fly and his constant eagerness to fly to any meeting or customer's job site to make sure things were going well was a big factor in his success.

Then the owners told him they were selling the company. At age fifty-five my father was apprehensive but they assured him that he would be kept on. After all, he was the top salesman, always had been.

The new owners said they didn't know anything about stock options. They kept him on but put a young man in as his boss who immediately wanted to see sales reports and even justification for flying his personal plane to job sites. He quit. He wasn't about to relearn or recast his job after doing it well for two decades.

He decided to move to Los Angeles. He would be near his two granddaughters, close enough to visit. Once he arrived he began looking for work. And, like all men of experience, he soon learned that he was on the downward side of experience: too much. He finally got a job with a tiny salary and the far expectation of commissions. He still maintained his curiosity about new things, however, and his love of aviation. I was busy and we didn't see each other that much. It seemed it was a Pelton trait, separated more by emotions than distance.

After he went to visit his mother and brothers in Vancouver I received a call from his brother Rod. Could I meet my father at the airport? He's having trouble walking.

I drove to Burbank and waited for him to get off the plane. They still used rolling staircases and after all the passengers deplaned I could see a large man in a houndstooth jacket blocking the exit. On either side were two stewardesses holding him up. He had a silver medical cane, the kind you rent in hospital supply stores, and he was having a hard time standing. I rushed up to help him down and he seemed more embarrassed than thankful.

He had been having spasms in his leg and arm muscles and now he was feeling a loss of strength. My father was six-foot-four and had always been around 240 pounds, and now that weight was making him tired. We tried to go flying and I discovered he was flying his airplane by pushing on the rudders with a stick. He drove his car the same way. He was losing the use of his legs.

The doctors did tests and the results were simple and conclusive. He had ALS, Lou Gehrig's disease, and there was nothing they could do for him. Denial, anger, acceptance, all came in the predictable order.

He bought a gun. I chastised him for buying a silly .32-caliber Beretta, which, I kidded him, would bounce a bullet off his thick head and probably kill an innocent bystander. He decided that he wanted to go home to be with his mother and brothers in Vancouver.

The doctors had given him a few months to live and I wanted my girls and maybe even myself to wring out every minute of time we had together, so we went too. We had CBs to keep in touch as he drove his car and I drove his van. When the twins would sit with him, they would ask questions about everything they saw. They were unaware of the short time they had with him and loved him dearly because he was always gracious and precise with his answers.

Not being fully experienced as a parent, he would call me on the radio and plead with me to swap them out, because he couldn't think of any more things to talk about. He and I also had our share of conversations. My father asked me if I would shoot him.

Life is full of tough decisions but none as tough as being asked to play God. My answer didn't come easily because either way it involved pain and a lasting memory of the consequences. I tried to see if there was anything to be gained by ending his life. Yes, he was about to suffer greatly, becoming in the next few months a childlike burden, with all the mental anguish that brings with it. But would it be merciful to put a quick shot into his brain, smashing in a bright flash of white light fifty-five years of conscious thought? The deed wouldn't hurt him but it would kill me and forever extinguish the resilient flame that kept me alive.

My decision was to give him the courage to use the rest of his life. I told him he had released years of anger, pain, confusion, and mistrust with the conversations we had shared watching the girls splash in the swimming pools of cheap motels along the way. I wondered if his mother, brothers, and sisters could benefit from the same soul-searching and conversations. I promised that when he felt he was looking at the end, I would deny life support and he could float dreamlike from lack of oxygen to sleep.

He seemed to accept that the son had become a father. The ride was through the fertile San Joaquin Valley in July and I remember the two red stripes of spilled tomatoes that fell off the overloaded produce trucks like bloodred lines leading me to my destiny.

THE MAN WHO DIED YOUNG

Vancouver, British Columbia · The call came a few months later. My father had died in his sleep. At first he had wanted to be cremated, then, when he had more time to think about it, he wanted to be buried in the place where he was most happy: Luseland, the small Saskatchewan farming town where he grew up. The day my father was buried was an ugly frozen day. The snow raged across the prairie and left no warm place unchallenged. They tried to dig a grave next to his father and grandparents but the ground was too hard. A farmer graciously offered to lend the use of his backhoe to finish the job. On the ground was a simple gray box that held the body of my father. The hard prairie wind had no mercy.

AND THE RAIN
BEGINS TO FALL

Sabah, Malaysia · I am in a small clearing at night in the Borneo jungle. The rain pours down in endless streams. How can the sky hold so much water for so long? My tears are masked by the water pouring down my face. I have carried a great sadness with me to this remote place and now I am trying to wash it out, leaving only the strong, dry bits inside. Sounds of tree frogs, insects, birds, and other nocturnal animals are almost deafening. The small fire sputters and hisses under the deluge. Occasionally a six-inch moth will fly out of the darkness and land on my face. They are soft, inquiring, and ultimately doomed to escape my curious grasp and leap into the fire. They distract me from the sharp jabs when I remember death.

It takes many nights like this to stop crying. Here in this great jungle, life and death are much simpler, much easier to deal with, much less painful.

The Ibans believe that the marks and tattoos a man earns during his life become sources of light after death. They guide him across the river of death and through the darkness to find peace. When he gets to the other side, his pain becomes joy and his sadness becomes happiness.

After a while I am cleansed by the heavy rain. My marks have darkened, ready to provide the light I need. I am happy soaked to the bone, a steaming, rank, muscular animal in the middle of primitive jungle. As the sun comes up high above and paints the sky a tired blue, I am content. I have learned how to cleanse myself, to rebuild from the inside out.

DIE LIKE THUNDER

Somewhere along the coast of California · I had just watched two men I loved die slow, lingering deaths. A third, who had influenced my early career, was also gone.

All died too soon. All had plainly pointed out that it was up to me to do what they could not. I had to harness my ambitions in my own fashion, to heed the vague force that powered me instead of fighting it. I did not have to explain that vision anymore. It was up to others to accept what I did and decide if they wanted to learn from it. My life's work was to leave something behind that would echo and resonate beyond a brief flash of light. It was time to live like the wind and then to die like thunder.

PART THREE

DARK
PASSAGE

THE ADVENTURE BEGINS

London, England · The morning dawns cold and blustery gray clouds scud across the Victorian rooftops. As I walk through Hyde Park, cavalry officers exercise their horses. I pass pale yellow daffodils and brilliant green lawns. The scene of blanketed cavalry officers along Rotten Row could almost be a hundred years earlier. I have chosen to start my trip to Borneo here in this gray place at the heart of adventure. Just as young people are thrilled by the launch of the space shuttle, a hundred years ago this was a place that stirred souls and sent adventurers into the unknown.

Ahead, across the park, is my destination, tucked between the red brick elegance of Albert Hall and the embassy recently damaged by the SAS counterattack on terrorists. The grim reminder that England's once far-off battles of occupation are now being fought by enemies in the heart of London disturbs my Victorian reverie. Things have changed.

As I make my way across the street, I see the stern, polar-clad statue of Shackleton tucked in an alcove of the building above. A statue of the great African explorer Dr. Livingstone peers inquisitively around the other corner from his niche in the wall. A simple sign on the red brick building tells me that I have arrived at the starting point for many of the world's great explorations for over 150 years—the Royal Geographical Society.

The society was founded in May of 1830 by a group of well-traveled London gentlemen who determined they would form a society "whose sole object shall be the promotion of that most important and entertaining branch of knowledge—geography."

Today the RGS not only has the best collection of maps, diaries, and artifacts from explorers but also runs an Expedition Advisory Center that stocks books on how to mount just about any kind of expedition you can dream up. I am here to find maps and information about the island of Borneo and to absorb some of the mystique of this hallowed place.

I had come here a few years back and met a lady who had been in Borneo. Fascinated by my expeditions, she had insisted I join the RGS. A few months later an official-looking piece of paper arrived:

Sir, I have the honour to inform you that the council have this day elected you a Fellow of the Royal Geographical Society subject to the conditions governing the completion of such Election as provided in the Bye Laws. I have the honour to be Sir, Your Obedient Servant . . .

I had no idea what that meant.

The map room is a musty room, walled on three sides by worn, leather-bound tomes. Faded black-and-white blowups of the Himalayas teeter on top of the bookcase. After a discussion of my needs with the director of the map room, I am led through the corridors under the gaze of past RGS presidents and British kings and queens to a reading room. Sunlight streams through the windows, illuminating a scale model of Everest. On the walls are stern, yellowed portraits of Stanley, Speke, Livingstone, Ross, Everest, and other notables. Inside this august institution that sent Franklin to find the Northwest Passage and Livingstone to find the source of the Nile, geographic endeavors are not taken lightly.

Every map tells a story and has a purpose. I browse through them, from the steel-engraved maps of early explorers to the computer-generated maps of today: ancient Chinese trading maps, Dutch and British colonial maps, OSS military maps of World War II showing navigable waterways and indigenous peoples. There are oil and mineral company exploration maps and the most recent aviation maps. More than just geographical indicators, the shifting borders, the names of discovered regions, and the increasing level of detail tell a romantic history of discovery. Each map shines a bit more light on this dark region. Most of the expeditions are purely scientific, looking at fish, identifying trees. Some are more grandiose. A new cave system needs to be mapped. Forest preserves need to be set up.

As I progress through the expedition reports and maps, I am heartened by the blank areas that remain obstinate blind spots. Even in this age of daily satellite imagery and helicopters, there is still too much cloud cover over Borneo to create an accurate map. I look up at my august companions in oil and am thankful that, yes, there are still wild places to explore and adventures to be had. I am not a soldier, an explorer a scientist, or even a journalist like the great explorers of the Victorian age. I am just curious and it remains to be seen what adventures await me. I will descend into the dark, nameless depths of Borneo, drawn like a moth to the bright white spots on the map. I feel that there I might be among my kind.

THE FACE

London, England · To understand the soul of the adventurer, you cannot just browse through his journals, notes, and maps. You have to look him straight in the face to find out why he made the hard choice between reading about adventure and living it. It is not surprising that, trapped on this small island and smothered by rules, class, and blandness, England's best have ventured into the most far-flung regions of the world. My next stop is the National Portrait

Gallery, a gallery dedicated to paintings, photographs, and sculptures of great Englishmen. Wandering through the hushed halls, I am greeted by row after row of austere pasty countenances of mid-nine-teenth-century England. Stern expressions, ill-fitting clothing, and dark suits are set against grim, gray backgrounds.

I climb the marble stairs to the third floor and there I find the reason for my visit. In a small room, out of the way and easy to miss, are portraits of the great English explorers of the Victorian era. An elderly, balding museum attendant sleeps peacefully under the fierce portrait of Captain Sir Richard Francis Burton. The errant linguist, much-maligned explorer, celebrated translator of *The Thousand and One Nights* and other "questionable" books, is one of my heroes. Whether it was boldly walking into the city of Harrar, where all white men were instantly killed, making a pilgrimage to Mecca, visiting the bloodthirsty kings of West Africa or battlefields in South America, Burton had an inextinguishable curiosity that was matched only by his contempt for Victorian society. The man produced an endless stream of tomes on everything from dueling, to exotic sexual practices, to gold mining; he also translated Portuguese poetry.

The small painting of Burton is more than a portrait, it is a statement. Burton's blazing countenance is not a mistake but a deliberate attempt by the artist to communicate the burning intensity of the man. Pea-sized globs of white paint have been added to his dark eyes to make them glare across the room. The physical size of the portrait is small, as befits Burton's legendary modesty. There are no monuments to Burton, no place-names, not even a tiny river named after this adventurer. It is a sobering thought to realize that most of his works sit idle in musty antiquarian bookshops and that only he understood the meaning of his thousands of adventures, loves, pains, sorrows, and joys. He paid a great personal price and left a new standard for personal exploration.

Across the doorway from Burton is a representation at the other end of the spectrum. An oversize, rather foppish, windblown portrait of a young Sir James Brooke, the rajah of Sarawak. In an effort to capture his fame and accomplishments, the painter portrays Brooke like a caricature from *Boy's Own* magazine. His boyish good looks and the breezy setting contrast sharply with Burton's dark, hard intensity. Brooke was to spend his inheritance on a well-armed ship and seek fame and fortune in the turbulent Far East. He found both. Through bravery, ambition, and a dash of trickery he became the ruler of Sarawak, master of a nation, and the first in a line of three White Rajahs who ruled uncontested until the realities of World War II ended their dynasty.

Two other portraits sum up the mood of the era. To the right is Lord Kitchener, standing fiercely in the deserts of Egypt, his bristling whiskers and intense stare betrayed by his soft schoolboy eyes. Next to him is Sir Robert Baden-Powell, founder of the Boy Scout movement, stiff and uncomfortable.

One last portrait graces the faded red flocked wallpaper. It, too, is of modest size and displays a soft-featured, balding man against a background of books, staring wistfully out a window. This is Rudyard Kipling, the man who wrote books about adventure and lionized the peculiar British trait of seeking adventure for its own sake. "The Man Who Would Be King," *The Jungle Book*, "Gunga Din," and *Kim* colorfully captured the feeling of exotic adventures in faraway countries.

This odd assortment of characters comprises the complete adventurer: Burton, the pariah of polite society; Brooke, the empire builder; Kitchener, the soldier; Baden-Powell, the creator of millions of little adventures; and finally, Kipling, the dreamer who turned hard realities and hard people into fascinating tales of adventure.

My pilgrimage to London has made me feel comfortable in what I am about to do. There is no prospect of wealth or fame ahead of me, only the satisfaction that I have to live a piece of my life to the fullest before complacency and age catch up with me. My silence is disturbed by the 747s on final approach to Heathrow. I look up. It is time to start my journey.

THE EARTH CALLS TOO QUICKLY

Somewhere in the Apo Kayan, Indonesia · The smell of leaking avgas is not a good omen. I check that the pilot and crew are okay and throw open the rear exit door. My first thought is to throw our exposed film as far away from the plane as possible in case of an explosion. As we throw our gear out the back door, the pilot and copilot sit dazed in the front. I have never been in a plane crash before.

Seeing the longhouses with the clearing by the river had been enough for us to think it was time to land. We had been flying for the right amount of time and we didn't have a choice. My early years of aerobatic flying with my father in his Citabria, and dozens of close calls with bush pilots in the Yukon, had removed my fear of flying. But, like they say, it's not the flying that kills you, it's what stops you from flying. Since we had the luxury of two pilots, I felt that if they said this strip was doable then that was fine with me. I got my first butterflies when the pilot set up for a full-power, full-flaps, combat landing. I climbed to the back of the plane and tightened my seat belt when I saw that the landing strip was actually made up of a cliff, a riverbank, and a tiny clearing. We hit hard. So hard that at first I thought we had done a "touch-and-go." I remember the equipment floating in the air in slow motion and then, as if we had hit warp speed, accelerating toward the front of the plane and smashing against the bulkhead. The sound of the bamboo hitting the plane echoed like a hundred baseball bats pounding on a drum. Roaring props smashed and shattered the wood into splinters as we careened into the forest. Waiting for the final sight of the front of the plane turning inward toward me, I was relieved to discover that we had actually stopped. The pilots screamed at each other to kill the battery, shut down the engine. They madly flipped switches and then sank into a long silence.

After our gear is out, we have time to review where we are. The plane is at a grotesque angle, resting a few feet from a large ancient Kenyah burial tower. We have been saved by the thick bamboo along the side of the narrow grass strip. The groves of four-inch-thick bamboo had beaten the leading edge of the wing and, more important, had bent to absorb the impact and slow us down. The soft earth had gripped the landing gear, destroying the front gear and trapping the rear. We are lucky, very lucky. (We were told later that the spirit of the elder chief entombed in the burial platform had saved us.) All I can think of are stories a Sabahan doctor had told me of cutting the fingertips off all of the dismembered limbs of crash victims and putting them in plastic bags so they could be identified back at the lab.

An old man appears. He has a toothless grin, a deformed or mutilated left hand, and a weathered *parang*. He begins to cut a length of bamboo into two-foot lengths. Calmly and methodically, without really noticing our presence, he stands under one of the engines, holding up his bamboo container to collect the leaking fuel. Only then does he nod to us as if we are waiting for a bus. The fact that he can be blown into a pile of wet jelly if the gas hits the exhaust pipes does not seem to faze him.

Gradually, more people from the village appear. Never having seen a plane of this size, particularly in this bizarre position, they peer under, over, and inside. Taking their cue from the old man, the villagers begin to cut short lengths of the thick bamboo.

Soon the ladies are placing pots and bamboo leaves under the fuel tanks while we run around hoping that nobody lights up a cigarette while waiting for the containers to fill.

The pilot is apologetic. I try to explain that any landing you walk away from is a good landing. He doesn't see the humor in this old saying, since he has just cracked up a very expensive piece of oil company property in a very remote place.

In our conversation with the villagers we find we are in the wrong village altogether. We try to persuade our audience into dragging the plane to a level area where the damage can be better assessed, but for some reason the tone of the crowd has become more serious. The local police chief has arrived. Acting stern and concerned, as all Indonesian police do, he is not pleased by our spectacular descent and miraculous survival. Why are we here? Who gave us permission? Who is responsible for the damage? The pilot and navigator sidle up to us and in soft voices tell us to walk slowly toward town, act stupid, and not answer any questions.

Something scared me on the fast ride down—I enjoyed it.

BLONDE ON BLONDE

Krakatau, Indonesia · The big Chinese catamaran is not riding the waves, it is piercing them. Twenty- to thirty-foot waves push the bow and then the back up as we slide down the killer waves. I am caught in a typhoon in the deadly focal point where Sumatra meets Java. My twin daughters are holding onto the steel supports and wondering if this is fun or the last day of their lives. Their perfect, cherubic faces register joy and fear. My wife is not happy—at all.

It was something that was promised to me but never happened. My mother told me that she would take me somewhere like Europe or Asia. Instead, at age ten, I was banished. My girls are now ten, an age I remember as being part dream, part reality. Like soft clay, even gentle impressions make lasting shapes. I swore that my children would have the things I never had. But there would be a message, a passage for each gift.

And so we are caught in a hellish storm on our way to explore the smoking volcano of Anak Krakatau. I feel no fear, it is not our time. My children sit comfortably in my strength.

We spent eight weeks exploring the world. In Sumatra we rode elephants, raced *becaks*, swam through pristine coral reefs. In the Seychelles we clambered up granite sculptures on uninhabited islands, learned to drink *lattes—con tante scuma*. In Kenya we camped in sweaty canvas tents. In Tanzania we stayed where leopards left footprints in the soft white sand, spent nights listening to hippos crunching the grass outside the tent. In Italy we learned about art when the wealthy encouraged it, cooking at its finest, and the general worn patina of culture.

Back home teachers tut-tutted that the girls had missed a lot of school, but they had learned more in two months than they had in the last ten years. I could see the difference in their eyes. I had passed on my burden and my gift. These two perfect girls would be wonderful women.

THE WHITE GHOSTS

Tawau, Sabah · I have made a friend. Michelle is half Filipina, half Spanish, and curious. Tall, thirtyish, more European in her features than Asian, a bewitching mix.

Over lunch I learn that Michelle works at the hotel where I am staying. She has been watching me. She tells me about her friend Jane. Would I like to meet her?

Jane likes to be called Jacqueline, her working name. Her real name is Jane Kate Lee. Like Michelle, she is half Spanish, half Filipina, with probably a touch of Chinese. She combines the best of all these traits. She is tall, shy, and beautiful. Slightly awkward in her height, she moves gently and sits lightly. Jane wants to be a fashion model and wears her clothes well. She would also like to get married again and settle down.

Jane works on and off as a massage girl in Tawau. She has a cell phone and is only a few minutes away when management calls. She makes enough to live in an upscale room at the Marco Polo, the swankiest hotel in town. It is a nice room on an upper floor with a view of the ocean beyond. She is trying to get out of the massage business but it is hard. She was married at eighteen and now has a five-year-old son. Back in the Philippines she met a man who offered her a good job in a hotel in Sabah. She didn't have a passport or a plane ticket but that would be taken care of by her new friend. When she got here, she found herself on the sixth floor instead of reception. The entrance to the sixth floor was clearly marked "Health Club." When she was told what she was to do, she was shocked. When her first customer came in and sprawled out naked for his massage, she cried and cried and cried. Her beauty saved her, though. Jane's looks brought her to the attention of one of the Kota Kinabalu gangsters that run the health clubs across Sabah. She became his eighth "wife." When she ran away from him, she hid out with a lawyer who wanted to marry her but she was not in love with him so she left him. Then she met an Australian who got her a passport and took her to Australia to live with him, but she gave him his ring back and returned to Tawau. Now her passport has expired. She cries. Michelle calls her whenever someone wants to have sex with two girls and they will pay M$200 for each girl. Jane also calls Michelle if she finds a high roller. They take care of each other.

Michelle explains the massage business. She tells me it's really quite simple. In Sabah, massage or health clubs are located on the top or bottom floor of business hotels. There are also discos, usually on the top floor of the hotel, where patrons drink their minimums and listen to loud music in almost total darkness. Here women of questionable beauty grope men's private parts in exchange for overpriced girl drinks. The darkness works both ways, since the Stygian ambience, along with the ear-splitting music, hides the men's nervousness. There are also karaoke clubs where hostesses will endure the off-key singing of their new gentlemen friends and arrange to meet later in their hotel. Often the men just enjoy the attention and are willing to pay the premium for the companionship. Karaoke girls are tolerated by local wives as a normal part of male nights out.

I convince Michelle to take me, Coskun, and the Turkish TV crew that is on the expedition with us upstairs and tape what goes on. Maybe it will help, maybe it will get her killed. She demurs. I ask her if she wants to make a difference. She agrees to do it.

The dorm is full of girls getting ready for the night's work. Instead of being embarrassed, they welcome us in. It looks like steerage on a ship, with underwear hung up like haphazard flags. There is not enough room for the girls to move around at the same time, so most stay on the beds. It reminds me of a chicken coop, just the minimum room required to sleep and to live.

All girls have quotas of sixty-five hours per week, seven days a week, from twelve noon to around two in the morning. They are expected to make about M\$3,000 (US\$1,200) a week and if they do not they have to pay the difference. Most girls do not meet the money quota, so they are forced to borrow money lent to them by their employers at 100 percent interest. Technically the massage parlors do not sell sex, since they do not charge for it. But the girls are forced to provide "extras" just to pay the difference in their quotas. These rules are posted on the walls of their cramped bunk bedrooms.

The other girls tell me Michelle is the top dog of the massage business. Watching the local news on television, she points out various politicians, businessmen, and other dignitaries she has accommodated. She knows them all. Michelle has a fifteen-year-old daughter in the Philippines. She has worked here for ten years and now trains all the new girls.

The girls' stories could have been xeroxed and handed out. Most are from small towns in Malaysia or the Philippines. Promised normal jobs in a tourist hotel, they were put to work in the health club with no way to return. Most owe more than they make. What little they keep they send back to their families, which ensures that they will never save enough to leave.

These girls are at the mercy of their employers and their ultimate owners, the Chinese gangsters. And it starts with the parents. Fathers in the Philippines sell their fourteen-year-old daughters to boatmen who promise to find them good jobs in Tawau. Like big-game hunters, men hired by gangsters hang around discos in these backwater towns looking for the most beautiful women. They are rewarded handsomely when they arrive back in Sabah with a new trophy. Gangsters play their own games when they go to discos and see potential trophies. They will slip three Valiums into a girl's drink and then that girl will wake up sore, abused, and with a large tattoo on her buttocks. The tattoo is the mark of the gangster girl. Branded like cattle or Grade A beef, she will never be able to marry in Asian society.

There are two kinds of girls that bring top dollar in Sabah: virgins and "freaky girls." Freaky girls are rented out by the gangster for Chinese parties. These uninhibited girls are worth M$500 a night. What is done to them is no concern of the gangsters. Many at the end of their careers are tortured and murdered for fun.

Virgins are worth M$1,000 wholesale and fetch three times that when sold to the end user. Although there is no shortage of virgins in the festering slums, it requires long negotiation with the parents and of course inspection to make sure you get the goods. Michelle seems to know too much about the procuring side of this business.

As Michelle and Jane tell me these stories, I realize that we are peeling away layers of truth like skinning an onion. The things that happened to somebody else are actually firsthand, and Michelle and Jane are becoming increasingly more scared because they realize that they are now in danger for telling me so much and allowing me to film. I didn't want to tell Michelle I have noticed the large tiger and rose tattoo that curls from above her pants into her untucked blouse.

Jane goes to the one Roman Catholic church every Sunday and wonders how she can get into the modeling business in a dump like Tawau. Michelle is going to Brunei to try to start over again and maybe meet a rich Bruneian. Meanwhile Michelle has a friend who wants two girls tonight and they need the money for the airfare. I give them the money for the airfare back to K.L. and to get their passport renewed, but I know they will not be going back. Jane's cell phone rings and they disappear into Ahmed's taxi like white ghosts.

END OF BUSINESS

New York, New York · When I was a young trainee copywriter, Bob MacAlear told me, "Never make your pleasure your job. You'll never be able to take a vacation from it." I ignored his advice completely when I took the money I had made in advertising and bought a publishing company.

In 1947 a former OSS officer named Temple Hornaday Fielding published a guidebook to Europe, entitled, originally enough, *Fielding's Guide to Europe*. Europe was in a state of destruction but there were still many attractions for the intrepid to visit. Temple liked to party, dress well, and live life to the fullest. His book was written in a conversational style with many painful puns thrown in.

Fielding's Guide to Europe became the best-selling travel guide of all time and Fielding even appeared on the cover of *Time* magazine. He moved to Majorca and hired underlings to handle the annual updates of his famous tome.

As can be expected, the enterprise lost its edge and other books came to the fore. Frommer focused on budgets and *Let's Go* focused on students. Soon Fielding's tiny empire was shrinking. Shortly before Fielding died he sold the series to William Morrow, who, in a rudderless fashion, proceeded to shrink it further. I stepped in to buy what I thought would be my next big career.

I had done some research on my own and become enamored with what I thought would be the world's largest business: travel. I saw a growing demand for travel as not only a business but an expression of an individual's uniqueness, a way for people who worked in dull jobs to do interesting things and find out who they really were. I was not interested in books, I was interested in what I called a gateway to information. I decided to create a series of multimedia experiences using sound images, words, and emotions to capture and convey the uniqueness of the world. But beneath all this cold planning was a desire to truly discover places and understand the dark corners. I was never cut out to be a publisher but I was intrigued by the gray-hair and bow-tie world of publishing. It seemed smart, paced, and permanent. But I was about to find out that I had chosen this timid occupation as an excuse to catapult myself back into my real avocation, something that could not be bought.

AT PLAY IN THE FIELDS
OF THE WARLORDS

Dyabakir, Turkey · I have a perverse fascination for warlords, men who control thousands of people and immense wealth outside of any real social structure. I wanted to meet a man who lives where East meets West, clan meets politics, and old meets new. I have come to the cradle of civilization, the uppermost tip of the Fertile Crescent, now torn apart by ethnic, political, tribal, and religious strife, to a warlord who holds back the heathen hordes here at the end of the empire. The Bucaks control Severik, the last safe outpost in eastern Turkey, and from there onward it is a land controlled by Turkish death squads, special forces, and Kurdish terrorists. Coskun will accompany me and along the way he will help me understand what makes this area so dangerous.

The western terminus of the Silk Road is actually a smooth asphalt black highway built by the United States. Buildings become cinder block and then simple stone as we travel eastward. The hills are ribbed and worn by the constant foraging of goats. Not much has changed here in a thousand years, and not much will change. We are in the domain of the Bucaks, an age-old feudal area in war-torn southeastern Turkey.

We drive up a narrow cobblestone alleyway just wide enough for a car to pass. There's a Renault blocking the way. Getting out of the car, we notice for the first time that there is a man behind a wall of sandbags pointing an AK-47 in our direction. The large house was built two hundred years ago and is lost in the maze of medieval streets and stone walls.

We politely explain who we are and why we have come. We had telephoned earlier and been told that no one was at home—an appropriate response for someone who has survived frequent assassination attempts from terrorists, bandits, and the army.

Out from a side door comes a large man with a pistol stuffed into his ammunition-heavy utility vest. He flicks his head at me and looks at Coskun inquisitively. He hears our story, recognizes Coskun from a year ago, when the photojournalist stayed with the warlord for three days. He smiles and gives Coskun the double-buss kiss, the traditional greeting for men in Turkey. He then grabs me by the shoulders, does the same, and welcomes us inside. We walk up one flight of stairs and find ourselves in an outside courtyard. We are joined by two more bodyguards. They're older, more grooved, hard-looking. Most of one man's chin has been blown off his face; it tells us that we should probably just sit and smile until we get to know each other a little better. We sit on the typical tiny wooden stools men use in Turkey. These have the letters "DYP" branded into them, the name of the political party with which the warlord has aligned himself.

The bodyguards stare into our eyes, say nothing, and watch our hands when we reach for a cigarette. It seems that Sedat Bucak, the clan leader, is out in the fields, but his brother Ali is here. We are offered *chai*, or tea, and cigarettes. The bodyguards do not drink tea, but they light cigarettes. One sucks on his cigarette as if to suffocate it.

When Ali finally emerges, he is not at all what one would expect a warlord to look like. Dressed in shiny black loafers, blue slacks, a plum-colored striped shirt, and a dapper windbreaker, he looks like an Iranian USC grad. That he and his brother are the absolute rulers of 100,000 people and in control of an army of 10,000 very tough men is hard to imagine, but when the armed men rise and bow, I believe it.

Not quite sure why we're here, he offers to show us a gazelle that he was given as a gift by one of his villages. The gazelle is kept in a stone enclosure and flies around the pen, leaping through doors and windows. We ask if we can visit with Sedat. Ali says, "Sure." He is out farming. The bodyguards bring out an arsenal of automatic weapons. Ali and his bodyguards get in the Renault and drive down the streets with the barrels of their guns sticking out the windows. I follow behind, wedged in between more swarthy armed men. Nobody seems to mind or notice. Even the soldiers and police wave as we drive by. The people just stop and watch.

Ali stops near a field where men, women, and children are picking cotton. Cotton needs water, and there's plenty of it. It also needs cheap labor, another commodity of which the Bucaks have plenty.

The people stand still as we get out of our cars. Ali tells them to continue working while we take pictures. They resume picking but their eyes never leave us.

The men decide this would be an opportune time to show off the capability of their arsenal. For one nauseating moment I have the impression they intend to gun down this entire village. Yet it is target practice that Ali has in mind. Boys will be boys. So we start plinking away at rocks, using all sorts of automatic weapons. We aim for a pile of rocks about four hundred yards away. We hear the sound of ricochets as the bullets hit the black boulders. Ali is more interested in our video camera. He plays with that while we play with his weapons.

When boredom sets in, we continue our journey in search of his older brother Sedat. We finally locate him about three miles away. I know who is in charge by the small army that surrounds the man. His bodyguards are not happy at all to see us. We are instantly engulfed by his men poised in combat stances. Ali introduces us to his brother, but we still have to state our case. Sedat recognizes Coskun, but instead of the kiss, we get a Western-style handshake. We introduce ourselves to his dozen or so bodyguards. They never let their eyes stray from ours.

Sedat is a soft-spoken man—about five feet six inches tall, sunburned, and suffering from a mild thyroid condition. He wears a faded green camouflage baseball hat, Levi's, and running shoes, as your neighbor might. He also carries a Glock 17 in a hand-rubbed leather holster. It is unsnapped for a quicker draw. He comes from an immediate family of five hundred Bucaks. They make their money by growing cotton and other crops they sell in Adana. And, it is rumored, by running heroin from Afghanistan to Istanbul, something their enemy, the PKK, also does. But not in Bucak territory.

The Bucaks have wisely aligned themselves with the current ruling political party, the DYP. Realizing that the Bucaks can deliver 100,000 votes goes a long way toward successful lobbying and handshaking in Ankara, the capital of Turkey. At the age of forty Sedat Bucak is head of the clan. A warrior and farmer by trade, he is now a sharp and shrewd politician. If he's killed, his younger brother Ali will take the helm. Ali is only twenty-four.

Severik has long been a battleground. The city was completely closed to all outsiders, including the army, between 1970 and 1980. During this period there was intense street-to-street fighting between the Bucaks and the PKK. Thousands of people were killed; the PKK moved on to choose easier victims. The Bucaks cannot stray eastward into PKK-held territory without facing instant death.

Throughout our polite conversation Sedat is never more than fifteen feet from his bodyguards. Men drawn from his army as personal bodyguards have the lean, sunburned look of cowboys. It is hard to believe that this gentle, slightly nervous man and his forces are the only ones in Turkey who have been able to beat the PKK at their own game.

Sedat can never travel without his bodyguards; neither can Ali. The bodyguards match the personalities of the brothers. Sedat's bodyguards are cold, ruthless killers. They're picked for the bravery and ferocity they showed in the last ten days of warfare. Ali's bodyguards are younger, friendlier, but just as lethal. Ali and Sedat carry weapons at all times. Their choice of weapons also reflects their personalities. Ali packs a decorative stainless-steel 9mm Ruger, and Sedat carries the drab businesslike Glock 17.

Some of the bodyguards wear the traditional Kurdish garb of checkered headpiece and baggy wool pants. Their pants, or *salvars*, appear to be too hot to wear on the sunburned plains. One of the guards explains that they work like a bellows and pump air when you walk. Others wear cheap suits. Some wear golf shirts; still others wear military apparel.

Ahmed, a chiseled, sunburned man who wears green camouflage fatigues, seems to be the chief bodyguard and likes us the least. He wanders over to our car and starts rummaging through the luggage and junk on the backseat with the barrel of his rifle. I deliberately left my book and articles there so that it would be easy to confirm that I am a writer. He picks up a Fielding catalog and starts flipping through the pages. When he sees my picture next to one of my books, he points and then looks at me.

We chat with Sedat. He is eager to present a positive image to the outside world. We have brought a copy of an interview he had just done with a Turkish magazine. In it, he proposes linking up with the right-wing nationalist party and, together, he says, they could end the Kurdish problem. Coskun suggests that such a comment could be taken as a bid for civil war. Sedat shrugs it off. We suggest getting some shots of him driving his tractor. There are few other farmers who drive a tractor with an AK-47-armed bodyguard riding behind on the spreader.

While I take pictures of Sedat on his Massey Ferguson, the guards bring out the *gnass,* or sniper rifle (*gnass* is Arabic for "sniper"). It is an old Russian Dragunov designed to kill men at four hundred to eight hundred meters. When I walk down to take pictures, Ahmed, the cagey one, slides the rifle into the car and shakes his head. He knows that a sniper rifle is not for self-defense but is used for one thing only. As they explain to us, "With this rifle, you can kill a man before he knows he is dead."

Hearing of how well we shot back at the cotton fields, Ali's bodyguards want to try their luck again. We blast off some more rounds at a Pepsi can they set up. Ali's bodyguards are having fun. Rifles are too easy. They then switch to handguns. We are all bad shots. No one comes close to hitting the Pepsi can. Then one of the bodyguards marches up to the can and "executes" it with a smile.

While Ali's bodyguards clown around with us, Sedat's bodyguards never move, or even take their hands off their guns.

After chatting with Sedat and nervously entertaining his bodyguards, we head back into town. There, we're taken to lunch at Ali Bucak's restaurant and gas station. We eat in Ali's office. The bodyguards act as waiters, serving us shepherd's salads and kabobs, with yogurt to drink. They serve us quietly and respectfully and eat with one hand on their guns. The SSB radio crackles nonstop, as various people check in. We talk to Ali about life in general. Can he go anywhere without his guards? No. What about when he goes to Ankara on the plane? They have to put their guns in plastic bags and pick them up when they land. What about in Ankara? They change cars a lot. Does he like his role? He doesn't have a choice. Does he like feudalism? No, but he doesn't have a choice. The government does not provide services or protect their people, so they must do it themselves. Who would take the sick to the hospitals? Who would take care of the widows? Since power is passed along family lines, it is his duty. He would like to know more about America but I don't think he would ever understand how different life would be for him.

As we eat, a storm comes in from nearby Iraq. Lightning flashes and thunder cracks. For now, everything is well in the kingdom.

THE TEACHERS

Somewhere in eastern Turkey · Kurdish children are not allowed to speak the native tongue in school, so schoolteachers are considered part of the colonial oppression against which the PKK is fighting. Teachers in Turkey are assigned to work for four years in eastern Turkey before they can work in the more lucrative cities of Istanbul and Ankara. Here, they are paid 8 million Turkish lira a month, about US$220. By comparison, soldiers get paid 35 to 40 million Turkish lira a month.

The teachers live in simple stone houses—one room for living and one room for sleeping. There is no plumbing; the bathroom is an outhouse about twenty yards from the house. But these conditions are not what makes this job dangerous. Over the last three years, seventy-five schoolteachers have been executed by the PKK. Schoolteachers in eastern Turkey are not raving political stooges of the government who spread torment and hate. They are bright college-educated people who teach reading, writing, and math. Many are just starting families and enjoy the work they do. The few who are dragged out of their houses at night, sentenced, and shot in the chest probably wonder what they did to deserve such a cold and uncelebrated death.

We spend the evening with two young teachers, a husband and wife, and their two young girls. The inside of the simple stone house reminds me of a bomb shelter: whitewashed, cold and damp. The house is lit with a single bare lightbulb hanging down from the ceiling. They share their food and are good company. After dinner we walk to the homes of the other teachers in this small village. Each family of teachers is happy to meet outsiders. There are two young female teachers who bring us cookies and tea, and there are two married couples, each with a small child. We gather together and talk about life in the war zone. Three days ago three teachers just northwest of here were rounded up, tied hand and foot, and shot the same way you would kill an old dog.

Many people feel that the teachers were shot because they had weapons in their houses. After the shootings the teachers from this village traveled to town to talk to the region's military commander and protest the arming of teachers as militia. The colonel greeted them as the protectors of the village. Taken aback, they explained that they thought *he* was the protector of the village. "No," he said, "it is much too dangerous to have troops out there at night. After all, I am surrounded by hundreds of soldiers, barbed wire, and fortifications as well as over a hundred trained antiterrorist commandos for backup." He offered the teachers one of each: a "big gun" (a German G-3) for the men and a little gun (AK-47) for the women. Not knowing how to react, the teachers abandoned their attack and glumly accepted the weapons and boxes of ammunition. They admitted to us they had no idea how to use them and were terrified that the children would find the rifles under their beds. They kept them unloaded.

As I walked back under a brilliant star-filled sky, I marveled at the ridiculousness of it all. Here we were with eager, youthful men and women—educated, enthusiastically discussing life and politics, sharing what little they have, and trying to make sense of it all. To think that a beautiful night like this could be interrupted by sudden death is unimaginable.

THE HIT MAN

Quezon City, Philippines · They say Nilo has killed over two hundred people, ten of them American. When I meet him, he seems like a nice guy.

We meet on the balcony of my high-rise hotel overlooking Manila. Down below, in the middle of a traffic circle, is a statue dedicated to a number of Boy Scouts who died in a plane crash. It also happens to be where Nilo shot the head of the CIA office. A lot of people get killed here.

I came to the Philippines because it is an odd mix of cultures and dangers. Here, Christianity, Islam, socialism, revolution, piracy, kidnapping, warfare, tourism, sex, corruption, joy, and hatred mingle. The fact that the most wanted man in the Philippines can join me for lunch at a tourist hotel says a lot about what is safe and what is dangerous here. You can glide gently through the tourist spots and never understand the fear, or you can take a wrong turn and end up dead or kidnapped.

The hotel employees' jaws slack noticeably when Nilo walks in. He is stocky, actually overweight, his hair graying in stripes. He looks comfortably nervous. He sits with one hand on one knee and leans in to listen. When he talks, he talks very quietly.

They caught him last year and charged him with fourteen killings. He says they will probably try to get him on about two hundred murders. They arrested his son and his daughter-in-law on trumped-up drug charges. He is the head of the Alex Boncayo

Gang, or Sparrows, the urban hit squad that dispenses justice for the little people. He is accused of executing Chinese businessmen, police chiefs, and a number of American servicemen. He shrugs the charge off but reminds me to describe him as the "alleged" leader of the Alex Boncayo Gang when I mention him. The police follow Nilo and his son all the time. Sometimes they even come to the house and bring doughnuts. He laughs. He hates doughnuts. Last time the police visited, his daughter-in-law asked the police to bring pizza.

His alias was/is Sergio Romero. He chain-smokes during our chat. I ask why he is nervous. He is nervous because he has people trying to kill him. He is also nervous about meeting me. Who am I and what do I want? I'm doing a travel show and want an interesting tour guide. Will we be doing a balanced story? he asks. "Absolutely not," I reply. He smiles. We understand each other perfectly.

Nilo's hit squad has merged with a guerrilla group called the RPA (Revolutionary People's Army) on the sugar-growing island of Negros, a union of a Maoist urban hit squad with a Marxist agrarian reform group that strikes back against landowners, police, and the military. Nobody has photographed this group and Nilo suggests that we visit with them deep in the mountainous interior. "Why not?" I answer.

The timing is not exactly the best. It is the thirtieth anniversary of the communist rebels and things are a little tense. The New People's Army (NPA) has kidnapped three military officers and things are jumping. I am also told there will be a number of attacks on March 29 to commemorate the anniversary of the NPA. The military is hunting down not only the group I am about to visit but groups in the south. It seems the government doesn't really want to eradicate the rebels but have them around to show that the government is doing a good job eradicating them. If there were no rebels, people would then focus on the government and wonder why things are so screwed up. Overall the military wing of the NPA has three thousand members. Mostly to justify their budgets, the Philippine military says there are at least seven thousand.

But back to the matter at hand. Nilo has never asked to be a tour guide and when he learns that he will be presented as a political rights activist in front of millions of people, he giggles.

He asks for a day to put things together, tells me he will send someone to meet me at the hotel. The next day two minivans with tinted windows show up. I suggest that we get a chrome jeep with a surrey top to see the city. He laughs. Why not? The most wanted man in the Philippines driving around in an open car.

Nilo asks that the Alex Boncayo Brigade headquarters be kept secret. It's in a bustling neighborhood with good escape exits. They pull out a big red flag for me to photograph Nilo against. There is a group of other young men who are not to be photographed. Seems they are the sons of affluent businessmen and college intellectuals and would be in a lot of trouble if Dad knew they were commie rebels. As in most countries it is only the rich and the destitute that can afford to be communists.

I get some shots of Nilo in front of his big red flag and we have a little chat to the sound track of schoolchildren across the street singing a Coke commercial. Then it's off on the tour. Our first stop is Senapa, the United Association for Landless—not a snappy name for a local basketball team, but a home to almost 100,000 people. The local chairman whips out statistics. This glorified squatters' city grows 5 to 7 percent each year. In 1987 there were only 7,000 families; now there are 28,000. The growth is blamed on simple biological reproduction and the bad economy in the countryside. This is a microcosm of the entire Philippines. A finite amount of land and jobs and rapid population growth typical to a Roman Catholic country. If only the pope had to change diapers.

The highlight of the trip is a visit to the Great Smoky Mountains. Not a national park, but a massive smoking garbage dump that doubles as a city. If you don't mind the stink and the filth, it's kind of a picturesque place. The smell is hard to describe but imagine what comes out of rainfall percolating through a thousand-foot-high pile of garbage. All along the base, the slopes, and the top are people picking through the trash. All the while a chain of dump trucks drives up and down, keeping the mountain growing. The people here usually have a specialty: cardboard, glass, plastic, or metal. The kids and women scramble up the steep sides picking and packing their specialty. The men carefully pack and strap the pickings to create tightly packed bundles worth pennies to recyclers.

I hitch a ride on a garbage truck to get to the top. It's an impressive site and sight. The only disturbing part is that people have built homes right at the base of the garbage, and rivers of fecal muck ooze by their front steps. The twist in this heavily politicized tour? The people choose to be here. Assuming that I am a developer, they send a man to tell me, "Don't evict us, we want to stay here."

Nilo has brought me face-to-face with poverty and injustice and the people choose to work it through by peaceful means.

Throughout the tour Nilo quietly chain-smokes and says little. His beeper goes off at regular intervals. He checks the messages carefully. It is his security people making sure that everything is clear. At the end of the day we sit and drink Pepsi. I ask him if he has seen much progress since the early seventies. He says no. Would he do it again? "Yes, I would do it again without regrets."

THE KIDNAPPERS

Tawi-tawi, Philippines · The Sulu Sea contains about five hundred islands sprinkled between Borneo and the southern Philippines. The Sea of Sulu was originally a sultanate when foreigners first came here five centuries ago. Now it is a place that sends apprehensive pangs of fear into any traveler's heart. You won't hear about many attacks on tourists because there aren't any. Not any attacks, no tourists. The region south of Zamboanga was a forbidden place for foreigners between 1974 and 1981. Even today foreigners are tracked like FedEx packages in the very likely event that they will be forcibly detained. Businesspeople are the primary target but average people are snatched for around 20,000 pesos. These days it's mostly military and business families who are affected by kidnapping.

The Chinese control 30 percent of the top one thousand Philippine businesses, so it's not surprising that the Chinese are the favored target of kidnappers. Another version of Chinese to go. So far this year 155 Chinese have been kidnapped, 15 of them killed because they could not meet the ransom demands. The Philippines is the only place in the world where kidnappers accept checks. The newest trick is to drive the victims straight to their ATM machine so they can withdraw their own ransom.

I am warned not to wander outside the hotel without a military guard, so I thank the security guard and hire a one-man trishaw taxi to see the sights. Heading up a scenic lookout, I stop at what looks like the monkey cage at the zoo. There is a forty-by-twenty-foot-long building with orange bars. I notice the brown hands wrapped around the bars. It is the local jail but the prisoners are not sullen reprobates. They wave cheerfully and call out "Hello, Joe," the common greeting for any Westerner in the Philippines.

I ask my guard translator who they are. He goes around and introduces each one by his crime: murderer, rapist, drug dealer, thief, etc. It would seem being jailed here is a pretty low-key affair. Some of the people jokingly call their crime "parental concern," a method by which parents can have their offspring jailed until they allow their release, thinking that a night in jail is probably good for reflection. Some of the men have been in for over two years. Not all are young.

Some of them are in their forties and their parents visit them every week. Surprisingly the men say they are happy in jail.

They show me around their tiny perches built of crates and cardboard. I point to the large clock on the wall and question its usefulness. "I can pray five times a day," says one enthusiastic prisoner. "I can rehabilitate myself," says another, smiling. "It is better for me to be here to learn how to be a better person," says a man from his bunk. I must be in a Lawrence Welk skit, I think to myself.

This would make sense if they were in a "country club" jail. But as I said, this facility is about as close to an animal cage as you can get, the major difference being that an animal would be better off. The prisoners have fashioned wooden platforms and boxes to alleviate the crowding. There is a chicken walking around one cell and in another is an old man dying in the corner.

When I ask my host if he is a guard, he says, "No, I am a kidnapper, but a good one." Explaining what he means, he tells me he tried to elope with his girlfriend but was arrested for kidnapping. He has been here two years awaiting arraignment. His girlfriend has married and never sees him. He has a college degree in agriculture. To pass the time, he teaches the other inmates. Today he is teaching Arabic so that the others can read the Koran. At this point I really don't try to understand but just listen.

The island of Tawi-tawi is crowned by a karstic structure with dramatic cliff faces. The island is surrounded by coral atolls and turquoise seas. I head down to the ocean to see the stilt villages. There, a young girl attaches herself to me. Not saying anything, just looking down shyly every time I look back at her.

The little girl is Marie Elena Tan, a ten-year-old who warns me that they will snatch me in a cycle taxi. "Do they use guns?" "No. Just a knife."

She offers to take me on a tour of the seaside village. Some men give me a dour look. It is clear that outsiders are not welcome in this community. I am too odd, too Western, too obvious. If I persist in chatting with them, though, they give me a smile. I can't help notic- ing the similarity between their gap-toothed sidewalks and their teeth. Most people have lost their teeth; even my young guide has blackened cracked stubs.

Marie Elena tells me there is much "stealing" here. Stealing is the word they use for kidnapping, usually locals or businessmen driven into the interior and held for ransom. I ask her to clarify. She tells me that the kidnappers are among the trishaw drivers. They pose as taxi drivers and pick up unsuspecting passengers. If they get a victim, they speed off to the interior villages, leave the hostage at a safe house, and then drive back into town to collect the ransom. I didn't realize how low-key and pervasive kidnapping is here.

"Oh yes, you must be careful."

"Would they kidnap me?"

"Of course."

"How do I know which taxis are the kidnappers?"

"They do not have numbers." She points to the registration num- ber on the back of a taxi.

I grab a trishaw and head toward a scenic village at the bottom of a mountain. I want to get some sunset pictures of a stilt village at the base of the massive limestone cliff. I am just in time for the sunset and my shots. The driver waits patiently. Afterward I tell him to head for my hotel. Strangely he points toward the mountain and takes a different route than the one from the airport. I assume he knows a shortcut.

Remembering that Marie Elena told me that the kidnappers do not have registration numbers, I look in vain for numbers in the dim light. Soon we are deep in the interior of the island and I cannot speak the driver's language. Am I being kidnapped? We emerge out of the dark forest into the nighttime clutter of a village. There is no elec- tricity here, just kerosene lamps. I am completely disoriented. I think of jumping out of the small tricycle but I am jammed in. I wait until he slows down, then I unsqueeze myself and bolt. Oops, I realize I have left my camera bag in the back. I return and my bewildered driver points to a hotel sign behind me. Same name, wrong village. I sheepishly get back in the trishaw for the ride to my hotel.

ONE AFTERNOON
IN BROOKLYN

Brooklyn, New York · Danger comes in many forms. I don't know why I sat at the table next to the only two girls in a bar on Saturday in Brooklyn.

One girl was dumpy with bad teeth, the other tall, elegant, but as tight as a guitar string. She wore black. I sat with my back toward the tall one and felt her stare at me. Even though I could not see her, I could feel her. Deep, slow, soft breathing. She was making me warm.

My meeting was paramount. A business deal with a publisher in a place chosen to expedite my onward flight to London. I had never been to this part of the world and I couldn't imagine I would ever return. Things like this are not supposed to happen in Brooklyn.

The meeting with the publisher was relaxed, fun, and productive. But I couldn't get my mind off the girl in black.

Whenever I turned around, she was staring. Her boisterous friend with the bad teeth broke the ice with a Brooklyn-accented glass-shattering nasal voice. Her opening statement made no matter. It was a question along the lines of "Where are you guys from?" Her friend was not chatty; she just stared deeply into my eyes.

Then as if orchestrated, the girl with the bad teeth went to the bathroom at the same time my publisher friend got up to get us another beer.

The tall vision from Brooklyn leaned over too far and asked me quickly and quietly, "Are you married?" She asked the question hurriedly as if she just wanted the words out of her mouth.

"Yes."

Her next question stepped on the first one. "Do you cheat on her?" My lips went to form the word "no" but my tongue stopped working. I had gone from spectator to player in a dangerous game. She sensed my hesitation and quickly got up from her stool and sat herself down facing me across the tiny, foot-wide table. I was a rat watching a snake, too fascinated to protest, too bewitched to see the danger.

Seeing, or rather feeling, her that close felt like afternoon sun.

She said, "Sit next to me," leaning in closer less to whisper in my ear than to increase her heat.

"Is there passion in your marriage?" She had probably rehearsed the first two questions but was now out on a ledge.

By now I am in slow motion, my brain trying to formulate answers, but the quickness of her questions does not let me reply. Maybe it doesn't matter what I say.

"I have just cheated on my husband but I broke it off. I never played around before. I only had three men before my husband. And now I have found passion. My husband is good to me but he doesn't turn me on.

"I know it's wrong. Should I marry this guy?" Her words are a torrent. She is only talking to herself. "I have a twenty-month-old kid. Kids are a drag. You don't know how hard it is with a kid."

There is nothing I can say. She needs to let it out, to find someone who cares but doesn't care. A stranger and a friend.

Thinking that if I just look concerned but distant I will escape unscathed, I stay silent. She stops midsentence, fixes her eyes on mine, and says, "You have incredible eyes. The most beautiful blue. You are gorgeous."

Bang, I'm dead.

She continues, "I broke it off last night. We only did it four times. It was good. Passionate. But I broke it off. Do you think he'll call me?"

Under her light makeup I see what I think is a bruise on her left cheek. Right-handed men leave bruises like that.

"He was in prison for two years. Just weed."

Her eyes are pleading with me not to judge her.

"I have wrinkles. See them?" She puckers her face and points to the bridge of her nose.

There are no wrinkles.

"I'm thirty and I have wrinkles. Is it wrong to want passion? Do you have passion in your marriage? My husband doesn't turn me on anymore. He's fat and I don't like that.

"I spin at the health club. I'm an instructor four days a week. That's where I met him. He wants to introduce me to his friends. Do I send out messages?

"Having a baby really wears you down. My baby was only five pounds seven ounces."

Her words come like rock slides bumping and banging into me. I get the jist but there's no place I can get a grip on what she wants, so I just stare back and hang on for the ride.

Whenever I sense that she is just talking to me because she has no one else, she interrupts herself and stares dead square into my eyes.

Luckily her friend returns and asks me if I am on business. Introductions are made as her strapping boyfriend walks in.

The publisher begins talking to the bad-toothed girl's boyfriend and they hit it off. Again I am left alone with the girl who I now know as Linda. My wife's name. She asks me my name.

"Oh my God, that's my husband's name. I'm a Taurus, what are you? A Leo. Oh God."

She continues to stare at my eyes and lips. Trembles of desire are shivering down her body. I can feel her leg as she presses tightly against me.

When the pupils of our eyes lock together, there is no mistake that we are joined in a very carnal communion.

"Am I good-looking?"

She bathes in my approval like an overheated runner in the surf. I am beguiled.

Linda whispers too closely, "You are gorgeous. When can we get together?"

Still, her conversation flip-flops between sensual and casual.

"You write books? I don't read much."

I tell her that within a few hours I will be on a plane. She doesn't care. She gives me her address but not her phone number.

"Follow me to the bathroom. I won't try to kiss you."

I get around to getting up to leave for my flight. She comes back. "I just phoned the baby-sitter. It's tough with a twenty-month-old. Men don't want you when you have a kid."

I disagree.

"No, men are picky. They are very picky."

First the chaste kiss good-bye but then, in a moment that defines people, she stops my lips and gives me the hard tug at the bottom lip with her teeth. As I pull away, her pain lingers.

Eleven hours later I am in London wondering what I was doing in Brooklyn.

THE INDIAN

Porcupine, South Dakota · I ambush Russell Means at his ranch on the Pine Ridge Reservation at nine o'clock. I didn't mean to. He thought we were supposed to meet at eleven. Driving up the rutted dirt on my black cop Harley, I had seen footprints of a man walking out. Strange. Now I knew why. Russell has been jogging. He has just flown back from shooting a movie on the Isle of Man. He plays Billy Two Feathers in a movie called *Thomas the Tank Engine*. I have to marvel that the world's most pissed-off Indian is now a movie star for kids.

Before Russell even goes into the dilapidated house to have a shower he starts his spiel. "We are in a concentration camp, a prisoner of war camp, an example of ethnic cleansing, genocide, and colonialism," all this before breakfast. While Russell has his shower his granddaughter makes us breakfast, traditional Indian hospitality. Russell likes being an Indian. His face curls into a sneer when I use the term "Native American." To Russell, "Indian" means *in dio*, or "made in God's name." You had better be up to speed with Russell.

It helps that he is famous—he is doing a lot of movie and TV work these days—but be careful not to believe too much of what you read about him. His film career started with the titular role in *The Last of the Mohicans* for director Michael Mann, then voice work for *Pocahontas* for Disney and *Natural Born Killers* for Oliver Stone. He would like to do more movies but he refuses to do the cocktail circuit in Hollywood. What's wrong with furthering his career by getting out and hobnobbing with the industry? I ask. "Fuck that," he says. Like I said, Russell is the World's Most Pissed-off Indian. I can't help thinking of Russell's Hollywood success as a direct correlation to Sitting Bull's celebrity in the Wild West shows at the turn of the century. I guess white folks like pissed-off Indians.

Russell's specialty is not just being pissed off, however, but getting out there and asking for it. "It" being the wrath of the entire American government. He is famous for a number of takeovers and flamboyant civil disorders ranging from the takeover of Mount Rushmore to the shoot-out at Wounded Knee in 1973.

Now I get the impression he is mellowing. He has recently purchased this thistle-choked land and dilapidated house built at the turn of the century. There is an abandoned pool, a tumbledown barn, and five horses that pretty much do as they please. Russell's satisfaction is that he bought it from a white guy who got the land in a crooked land deal.

Russell is a little more reserved after breakfast. He even has a sense of humor. "I pissed on Washington's head, you know." He is talking about the time he spent at the top of Rushmore, a place that desecrates the sacred Black Hills of South Dakota.

Russell is a hard man to read. He operates on three planes of existence at the same time. His game face is that of an Indian spokesperson who defends his people in front of the media. Complete with trademark leather braids and buffalo-bone choker. Then there is the militant Russell, a man who has taken up arms against the U.S. government. A man who has been jailed, beaten, and vilified for defending his peoples. And then there is Russell the celebrity, Chingachook, the badass Indian, the voice of Powhatan in Disney's *Pocahontas* ("I did it because the white guy marries an Indian woman"). A man who pauses between your thoughtful question and his answer, and then for half an hour vilifies your race and heritage for being uncaring and insensitive.

Russell's physical appearance is not that unusual on the reservation. Most Indians that have survived past the age of fifty are battered, scarred, and weathered. In fact they remind me of Afghans: bashed noses, crooked fingers, scarred ridges, smashed teeth, and deeply weathered faces are for the lucky ones. They are still alive. Many Indians die from diabetes, childhood diseases, drunken car wrecks, fights, and a list of other ills accorded only the very poor and desperate.

In the midst of the rich heartland is a nation of people that lives ten to twenty years less than their white American counterparts. The most dangerous place in America.

Russell wants us to rethink what we know about Indians, starting with the very image he has adopted: the Brave Indian Warrior look. "The warrior tradition is a romantic lie," he sneers. "Other than a few young and foolish men testing themselves, the Indians lived in peace until the white man came." He boils it down to the Indians being a matriarchal group compared to the patriarchal society of the white men. He says the Europeans have it all wrong. "The Indians had their shit together. The Indians won every military confrontation against the whites but were deceived by treachery." He points out that you only sign a peace treaty if you can't win a war. "If the United States won, then why did they force the Indians to sign peace treaties? The reservations were reserved by the Indians because they won."

I don't have the heart to tell Russell to just look at the poverty and desolation around him. Maybe he should take a tip from Germany and Japan. They should have lost.

I don't agree with Russell's view of Indian history but I let him range widely in our conversation. It sounds as if he is testing how ideas sound, as if the very process of speaking will help him zero in on what is the right message. He responds to my disbelief in some of his statements by assuming that "white men" or "Europeans" cannot comprehend the nonlinear, circular thought process of the Indian. He covers everything from ballot stuffing to racism as the reason for the Indians' failure.

Even mundane questions spark anger. He won't reveal his Indian name. "That's not germane to this interview" is his response. I am guessing "Crazy" is one of the adjectives.

Russell has carved himself an island where only he is right. Hollywood is racist, full of Jews, Indians are lazy and corrupt, the government is evil and stupid, the country is a disgrace, white men are brutal. He even complains his biography was about twice the length but was cut back by the publisher. Strangely enough, you won't find his bio, *Where White Men Fear to Tread,* in any of the tourist shops that hawk Indian and cowboy history and trinkets around the Pine Ridge Reservation. When I asked a graying matron at Wall Drugs why they didn't stock his book, she rudely said, "Nobody asks for it."

It may seem that I would dislike Russell but I like him a lot. We have a lot in common. He knows that only the most extreme players get even a mild mention in the media. He also knows that his war is not about him—it's about making people pay attention. Russell was meant to be a *shuhuda*, or martyr, like every other great Indian leader before him. But that has been denied him. Instead he is a healthy father and grandfather, a successful actor and recognizable celebrity. Sometimes life just doesn't work out the way it's supposed to.

In another place, for another cause, he would find his true position. Here, he is a whirling vortex of confusion and darkness trapped by his Indianness. Even his body language cannot hide his anger. An aggressive, head-back, chest-high, bowlegged walk. An intense stare as you listen. His very look taunts you to argue with him.

Toward the end of the day he realizes that he has been asked to run free and allowed to take us intellectually and physically where he wanted to take us. He has survived. His demeanor changes. His face softens. I offer to hook him up with any rebel groups he finds interesting. "That would be cool," he says.

When the sun goes down and the smell of the grass washes over us, he asks me quietly, "Did you get what you wanted?"

TV LAND

Custer, South Dakota · After leaving the Pine Ridge reservation I am given word that we are to cease and desist from shooting the show. It seems the president of the Travel Channel has seen the first rough cut and is apoplectic. I have been on the road and made the fatal mistake of letting the editor put together the show as he sees it. His first attempt was a stunning visual montage of a crucifixion. Artsy and rather cool in a dark way.

The president calls my exec producer partner Rasha late at night and expresses his disappointment at what he sees. "Can you imagine how upset the ambassador to the Philippines will be?" The show features interviews with an assassin, rebels, pirates, hit men, cops, and prostitutes. It is not something they would air on the Discovery Channel. When I return to L.A., I expect to be fired. I am not. They want more of a story line. I make it look too easy, bouncing from one deadly group to another. They want me to be the hero. The budget is upped and I get back to work. Funny business, this Hollywood.

THE COWBOY

Lewistown, Montana · The Cowboy Poetry Fair is three days of crusty-looking cowboys and cowgirls reading poetry in a place where you find $500 hats and $25,000 saddles. The poets are a blend of city slickers with carefully faded clothing and retired ranchers. An older man with the soft thick fingers of a rancher comments on my Afghan *desmal.* "That sure is a pretty scarf." "You a poet?" I ask. "Sometimes, when people let me," he says, and softly chuckles. I like him immediately.

He is here to sing a few songs and read a few poems.

He was born on a ranch and worked some of the big outfits. In the "middle passages" of his life he started his own operation but couldn't make a go of it. He works at a few jobs and comes to these poetry things to sell his tapes and read poems. He tells me that the West is over. There's a few cowhands punching cows, but with the price of beef and the price of land it's all over. I watch him sing his songs. He spends most of his time complimenting the other singers and poets. After his set he packs his guitar and harmonica and goes to play at a local restaurant for a free lunch.

He told me his poems are a little sadder than most.

COWBOY UP

Seward, Nebraska · The last float in the Seward Fourth of July parade is a flatbed with young skinny cowboys wearing colorful leather chaps and tightly creased black hats. The classic chiseled look of the rodeo cowboy lit by the hard prairie sun. Not too tall, light blue eyes, brush-cut hair, big hat, and that lanky walk that is aggravated by broken-in boots, tight jeans, and leather chaps, that uniquely American mix of country-western, cowboy movies, and cigarette ads. They wave and goof around drinking Bud Light and giving out rides to little kids on a tiny rocking bull. Two well-worn but young gals are also on the float. One has a tattoo that circles her biceps: "Rodeo Gal." They invite the crowd to come to the bull ride tonight to see the World's Most Dangerous Sport. How could I refuse?

At the fairgrounds the light is becoming a soft yellow backlight but is still hard enough to lighten all the colors. The dust dances in its shafts. The flag is backlit. The cowboys squint. Belt buckles sparkle. The first job is to load in the bulls. Furious brown, black, and tan behemoths that weigh between sixteen hundred and two thousand pounds are kicking and snorting in the cheap pipe corrals. They smash the pipes and flick their horns trying to catch anyone that walks by. The ends of their horns have been sawed off but the bulls have polished them with all their banging and gouging.

The second order of business is to get ready for the show. The cowboys limber up, practicing that classic twisting motion that bucking bulls bring on. The bullfighters, the appropriate word for the clowns who are the first to suit up and don makeup, wear loose cutoffs and brightly colored shirts to attract the bulls. They also carry scarves to wave in the bulls' faces. The makeup in this show is superficial. A cross, flag, and a few patches are daubed on. Their job is to attract the attention of the bull once it has thrown the rider. The trick is to calculate the bull's speed, run far enough ahead of it to get it going, and then cut back to the side of the bull. The animal just can't turn quick enough to snag you. Then it's just a matter of waving it into the side entrance and back into the corral. One of the clowns is a former football star who can really use his speed and dexterity in this job.

The older men who run the show are Marlboro men. Crisp white hats, deeply cleft chins, chiseled jaws, perfect creases around the eyes, well-trimmed triangular mustaches, and Ray Bans. They get things ready in that cool cowboy way. They stay focused while the younger riders go through that religious moment between getting on the bull and coming out of the gate. These men watch to see that they are ready and then pull the gate. But even these pros have to hightail it out of the ring and up on the fences when the bull spots them.

The announcer in the whitewashed fairground stand is playing country rock to get the crowd wound up. "Are you ready to rodeo?" he yells. A cheer goes up. "Let's rodeo!"

Bull riding is about the closest thing to feeding Christians to the lions we have these days. There will be injuries and there will be pain. There is a measurable sense of tension with the cowboys. They tape their wrists, tighten their spurs, check their chaps, limber their muscles. Each finds a quiet corner to pump himself up. Some pray. Most of these men are from Texas, a place where bull riding is not so much a sport as the measure of man.

The rules for bull riding are pretty simple. You hold onto a rope loop with one hand and only one hand. Touching the equipment, the bull, or yourself with your free hand, or using the free hand to hang on (or double-grab), will result in a disqualification. Women can use two hands to hold on with but will receive a 10-point deduction from their total score. Two judges each score 0 to 25 points for the bull's power and bucking pattern and 1 to 25 points for the rider's form, control, and spurring action. The maximum score is 100. If you survive and even win, you get a nice trophy and a few bucks.

It's time for the first of twenty-six bulls to begin. The bull handlers prod and smack the bulls into position. They slam and bang against the tight cages. Cowboys lower themselves down gingerly. The second the bull feels something it smashes against the sides. Handlers make sure everything is snug and safe. Much of bull riding is knowing the bull you will draw. A bull can be a spinner, a welly, a double-kicker, a union, a slinger, a head thrower, or hopefully a money bull, the kind of animal every cowboy wants to draw. Some bulls will be arm jerkers, crow hoppers (stiff-legged jumpers), slingers (bulls who try to catch your face with their horns), chute fighters, or worse yet, hat benders (just running), bloopers (no bucking), dinks, or Bufords (tamer bulls that just run around making you look bad and lose you points). You don't want to draw a honker, jump and kicker, one that sucks backs or is rank. These are evil bulls with no chance of delivering an eight-second ride, just a lot of pain when you are off the bull and on the ground. Cowboys can kiss the bull (a face smash), be freight-trained (run over at full speed), go out the back door (bucked off the back), or be dropped into the well (the inside of a spinning bull). If they get nervous, all they have to do is bail out by loosening up on the grip and leaning their weight against the bull. He will throw you a few feet into the air and then you land on your ass. All bull riders get hurt, it just depends how bad. There are three medical personnel standing by, an ambulance and a gurney. The doctor and the paramedics wear crisp turquoise cowboy shirts, black Stetsons and black jeans, and sunglasses. The only difference is that their pockets are filled with surgical tools that glitter against their jeans.

Cowboys who haven't felt the weight of two thousand pounds on their chest or innards scoff at padding. Those who have won't go out without equipment. A paramedic points out a good-looking young cowboy as an example of what can happen. He had his nose hanging off his face last year. The cowboy tells me that they had to throw away pieces of his nose and rebuild others—they couldn't find all the bits after he was kicked. They put it back together pretty well by the look of the red scars and white tissue, but it's a little delicate. He still rides but he wears a face mask now. He has shin splints in his wrist, he tells me. How long before it heals? "Whenever I stop riding." I wish him luck and tape his next ride. Within ten seconds he's back. The bull has stepped on his foot. The tough, cool, grown-up look is replaced by a child's look of pain.

I begin to dig bull riding. I want to give it a shot.

The organizer wisely won't let me ride a bull. He figures I am a little too big for a bull rider, but I can get up on one and feel what it's like. The experience of sitting on a bull is an interesting one. The bull feels massive and soft, but with plenty of muscle under the skin. It also feels damn angry. As soon as I put my weight on the bull, it tries to crush my right leg against the white steel rails. I try again and this time it pins my leg heavily. Turning its head as far as the cage lets it, the bull looks upward with an angry eye. Fuck you too.

PART FOUR

THE
PASSIONATE
PILGRIM

THE QUESTS

Redondo Beach, California · It's a perfect southern California day, glistening green palms against an achingly blue sky. Here we would say, "It's a Harley day," as hundreds of old paunchy men with salt-and-pepper beards *thraaaap* their way on too-shiny motorcycles along the coast and up my street. The parade outside my oceanfront house continues as anemic joggers, Day-Glo-clad cyclists, and lethargic dog-walking oldsters enjoy a sunny Sunday in February on what should be the dead of winter in America.

Leaving the lotus land of southern California for the third world is difficult but it provides the most contrast. In this idyllic, affluent spot, those who have the most, care the least. You can only appreciate heaven if you have made the descent into hell. No one is forcing me. I have taken it upon myself to visit the longest-running wars on three continents. My first visit will be to rebel leader Francis Ona on the island of Bougainville.

Francis Ona and I have an interesting nonrelationship. We both think we know who the other is but we have only communicated through middlemen (or women). Francis has been a little paranoid since the Papua New Guinea (PNG) government tried to kill him after he returned from peace talks.

Francis Ona is the leader of the Bougainville Revolutionary Army. The BRA shut down a large copper mine because the runoff was killing the island. The first eco war was started with rusty shotguns and slingshots.

Bougainville is a small island to the east of Papua New Guinea. Once high-yield copper and silver deposits were found there in the 1960s, the island quickly changed from primitive backwater to developed suburb. Until then the island consisted of villages run by chiefs who had very basic ideas on not only democratic process but the concept of landownership. They viewed land as something that is owned by all, and rules as something created and maintained by all. Not surprisingly the island now has a few problems with crime and dissension. When the mines were first dug, the mining company chose the most violating form of development, open-pit mining, which caused mountains of deadly chemicals and effluent to block pristine streams. This work was done by "rusties," lighter-skinned PNG workers. Gaining ownership to the land above the mine had been a simple matter of giving a compliant chief a few drinks and a lot of money and making him sign a simple paper. Cash quickly erased centuries of tribal ownership.

The Panguna mine on Bougainville, which Francis and his BRA shut down, provided about 45 percent of PNG's revenue and was just one of many mines set to rip into the pristine environment of Bougainville.

This was, in a microcosm, the story of America, the rejection of a colonial power, a test case for tribal rites over Western law, and a litmus test for what will become of the last wild places.

In earlier times Francis was a surveyor and a high-level mine employee. When he learned about the plan to relocate the residents of Bougainville to Australia, their land literally dug out from under them, he resigned in protest. He went to work as a truck driver and then as a cleaner helping to photocopy private documents. The revolution was long in coming but when it came the mine shut down and the island was quickly blockaded to starve the rebels out. The problem is that the Bougainvillians are resourceful and industrial. The Bougainville Revolutionary Army is a fairly cohesive, well-trained group of ex-military and nonmilitary fighters. Their biggest problem is getting enough guns. They started by digging up old Japanese weapons left from World War II and cleaning them up. Then they began making zip guns using galvanized pipes. When the fighting began in earnest, they would ambush government soldiers and then steal M-16s from them. There are also rumors of guns being purchased with bales of New Guinea Gold, some of the most potent *sensimilla* in the world, and the favorite of Australians.

The BRA were true jungle fighters, living off the land and occasionally appearing in Gizo as slightly bored and nontalkative teenagers looking for a Solbrew and a little R&R. As I am later told in Gizo, you can tell the BRA fighters because they are the ones who don't wear the green camouflage jungle fatigues.

From what I have learned from the handful of people who have met the rebels, I will try to slip in from the rebel supply base of Gizo in the western Solomons before a cease-fire takes effect in two months. There is just one problem. Well, actually there are three problems: I will be going in to find Francis Ona before the cease-fire is supposed to start, Francis Ona does not want to be found, and there will be more than a few people trying to keep me from getting there.

Just before I leave, another problem crops up. It seems Francis and his people are convinced that I am a white mercenary being sent in to kill him. One of my books' contributors was asked by a mercenary outfit called Executive Outcomes to assist in doing something that would contribute to Francis's demise. Naturally he said no, but the rumor spread its way to Francis, who has every right to be paranoid of white men bearing gifts, particularly ones from the mercenaries of Sandline International and Executive Outcomes, who tend to bring Hind gunships, infrared spy equipment, and a lot of nasty gizmos for killing.

Francis attracted me because he is an ordinary man thrust into an extraordinary circumstance. He is a former surveyor, truck driver, and now not only the leader a rebel group but a founder of a new country. Not a bad career. The story had a nice PC ring to it and wasn't being covered by the press. Originally I thought it was because nobody other than three other people had managed to get in. I was wrong.

LAST STOP

Choiseul airstrip, Solomon Islands · The big uniformed islander towers over me, standing too close. At this distance and with his height I am eye-to-eye with something hanging from a chain around his neck. Staring closely at the small white object, I realize it is a human tooth.

Shouting over the buzz of the Twin Otters' propellers, the blue-uniformed policeman with an unpronounceable last name on a cheap plastic name tag is telling me that we must leave the country on the same flight we just came in on. I have come to the most remote island in the Solomons. A blue and white paradise within sight of the dark blue island of Bougainville to the north.

It turns out that the yellowed molar belongs to his father. I have an overwhelming desire to ask the hulking barrier to my arrival if it was the only part he spit out.

This event is documented by an ABC News crew sent to travel with me on my voyage to the world's longest-running war zones. The director tasked with following my illegal meeting with a rebel leader videotapes the encounter surreptitiously. Jay, the director/camera-man, is relieved. Both he and the talking head had already told me that they would not be going with me to Bougainville. They had decided it was too dangerous. I will be making the attempt anyway.

THE TURN OF THE TIDE

Redondo Beach, California · Nine months after my attempt to get to Bougainville with a mercenary and a film crew from ABC, an eight-page handwritten letter arrived from the rebels but it was postmarked Northern Suburbs, New South Wales.

> *Dear Sir*
>
> *We have received your letter by fax from Rosemarie Gillespie. We did not respond at the moment of receiving your request because at that time we put on a policy to strictly ban all media from meddling in our affairs. The 9 years desperate struggles against monsters have taught us invaluable insights. We do not trust any foreign media. They were only making millions from the blood of both Bougainvillians and Papua New Guineans.*

The letter goes on to compliment me on my intentions and requotes passages directly from my original two-page fax. Finally Francis's secretary writes,

> *[we] can assure you that what ever you publish in your preliminaries will gain you access to Bougainville to see our President Mr. Francis Ona. I will eventually introduce you to him to accept your coming over to Bougainville.*

As Joseph Conrad put it best: "The tranquil waterway leading to the uttermost ends of the earth flowed somber under an overcast sky seemed to lead into the heart of an immense darkness."

My journey had not gone unnoticed. I had planted a seed and now I was to reap its fruits.

HEAVEN AND HELL

Arawa, Bougainville · Where is heaven? I used to ask in school. The nuns would point upward as if there was something that only they could see. My questioning of this was one of the main reasons I was thrown out of grade two. But here in the most elevated place in Bougainville I might be in heaven. A young boy leans over and drinks from the stream. In front of me soft clouds caress the mountaintops as they spill over into the valley far below. Volcanoes smoke in an air of impending primal change. The weather is soft. Down below I can see the crystal waters and white sand beaches. I am in the Holy Land, or Mekamui. Or at least that is what Francis and his people call it. Behind me is where the helicopters would land with armed men and attack the villagers. They would then burn their houses and kill the wounded.

I climb above the mine until we can climb no more. A simple white wooden cross on the promontory above the mine denotes that this is a Christian village. Today three thousand people live in Guava. Guava means "hole" in the local language of Nasi oi. The village did not get its name from the mine but from a small cave about half a kilometer away. The man that meets us is an older, bearded man who wears a faded red Umbro sweatshirt. He has a twinkle in his eyes and welcomes us to Guava. His name is Phillip. He is happy to see me. He has followed my quest and is proud to welcome me to the home of Francis Ona. He is very excited to meet me.

I wait while he arranges for my accommodations. I feel like I just arrived at a Palm Springs resort. Soon gaggles of small boys come out of the jungle and up from the village. They have tiny slingshots around their necks and keep their distance. Perhaps they have never seen outsiders. Perhaps they have seen outsiders. Either way outsiders have never been good news here. But a wave and a smile break their frozen stare. They press closer and biff each other to get a better view.

Phillip asks for my luggage, and my bags quickly disappear with the tiny porters. He offers to take me on a tour. In the formal jargon that Phillip adopts he tells me that "the president is indisposed but will meet with us tomorrow." His official tone makes me want to pretend to have my social secretary check my calendar to see if I am available. We walk along a stony path that overlooks the village. He explains the village has been rebuilt, that Francis's village was the first to be burned down. He tells me that it is good because it taught them to be self-sufficient. They have jungle medicine, a defense force, a government, everything they need.

Had Phillip been wearing an ambassador's sash, he would have fit in perfectly. Instead he is wearing the grubby torn red sweatshirt, tattered pants, and flip-flops. It is easy to write off the rebels as T-shirted optimists but there is some substance to his claims. They have fought and won a war over the last ten years. These people are above all resourceful and determined. So I do not scoff at Phillip's claims. Faith, ambition, and previsualization is, after all, how all great things are achieved.

The rooms are ready. A two-story house made of scrounged items from the mines. On one wall is a statue of Mary, the Ten Commandments, and a 3-D depiction of Jesus. In the bookshelf are tattered magazines and books. The only books in good condition are Bibles in pidgin. One man asks me if I can send books. They like *National Geographic* so they can teach the children about the world. These are eager intelligent people who constantly apologize for the conditions they live in.

Although they have suffered much, they are not angry. They are firm about going it alone. Peace on their terms. Independence on their terms. The others will learn. Bougainville must be for Bougainvillians.

I meet Francis the next day. He is a soft-spoken man who invites me to conduct a formal interview looking down on a blue ocean and wispy clouds. Surrounded by paradise, watching children put hibiscus flowers on an aged white cross, I imagine that it would be difficult for most talking heads to discuss constitutional mandates, military strategy, and global politics with a bearded man who is built like a brick shit-house—although in this case one that is carved from ebony—and wearing faded cutoffs and a grubby T-shirt. It would be even harder for them to remember to say "Mr. President" when addressing him. Strangest of all might be trying to understand why I had spent two years trying to meet him.

Today Francis is living proof that one man can fight back against big business, governments, mercenaries, and the forces of evil. He is the embodiment of the true strength of politics—that people can still shape the world.

Francis and his people want to live on their land in harmony, with their children, to drink from the streams and grow their crops in their soil, a sentiment I understand, since I was the one that coined the phrase "If you want to make a native poor, give him a T-shirt." Francis and his village would by all accounts be wealthy if he had just negotiated a nice settlement with the mine at which he used to work, the mine that was poisoning his earth, but there is no amount of money that could replace their land.

After they shut the mine down, hundreds of people were out of work and, from the outside world's point of view, their island was plunged into poverty. But was it? "The people have learned to exist without outside things. If you cannot survive without needing lights, phones, cars, fuel, jobs, television, are you not a beggar?" Francis was right. I had been to too many places where the once proud people gathered around cheap televisions, eating canned food and wearing tossed-off, secondhand clothes. People who once claimed the world around them as their friend. People who had been united in family, religion, work, play, and spirit but were now resigned to working in factories, surviving in soot-choked air, and wondering what went wrong.

Francis took great pains to show me that the Bougainvillians can survive without the outside world. "We will take what we want and disregard what we do not need. There are schools, medicine, music, clothing, and laughter."

I wanted to meet Francis because I assumed that all rebels have darker motivations, backroom deals, or burning hatred. Francis had none of these. It is only when one of the bright orange-painted Australian Hueys flies by that conversation stops and his jawline tightens. He is a man who wants to be left alone, to live his life the way he wants, a man who is not intrigued by the trinkets and promises of outside forces. A simple man and a complex man, of both violence and humor, who is building a country from the ground up. A believer in the power of people, of innate goodness, and of a spiritual force that will prevail over evil machinations. It saddens me to think he is ultimately doomed to failure, for I have found that countries do not spring from the fertility of the ground or the purity of their people, they are imported, packaged, laid in place, and enforced by outside business interests.

That I am the first outsider he has talked to in two years doesn't faze Francis or me. We were destined to meet. The man who made a country and the man who was determined to find him.

JUDGMENT DAY

Kampala, Uganda · Nairobi had an air of danger I hadn't noticed last time. People took taxis to travel even a few hundred yards. Guards stood outside every hotel armed with two-foot sections of rubber hose. Someone tried to snatch Rob's watch while he leaned his arm out of the taxi window. We were going over thirty miles an hour at the time. I was glad to get to Uganda, where the pace was noticeably slower, the people rounder, the trees softer, the colors richer. The altitude turns the equatorial heat into a comfortable warmth. English anachronisms exist in harmony with colonial disaster. The first thing you learn is that Uganda's beauty is marred by having too much history.

The first European to visit Uganda was John Hanning Speke, who spent a considerable amount of time in 1862 with the king of Buganda. In his effort to outdo Burton, Speke stayed to understand the lifestyle of this isolated Central African people. Then more morally focused Henry Morton Stanley came by and the king was so impressed with the Welsh American reporter-turned-adventurer that he asked him to send some teachers back to his country. For some unfathomable reason Henry sent Anglican missionaries, who arrived two years later. Since then it's been pretty much downhill, so it's probably better to cut to 1962.

In 1962 Idi Amin became the army chief of staff under Dr. Milton Obote, a former schoolteacher and the prime minister of Uganda under independence. As both Milton and Idi figured out how politics worked, money began disappearing from the treasury at an alarming rate. When the attorney general wanted to know where $5 million in defense bucks went, he and his wife were found dead. When Milt went on a junket to Singapore, he found himself permanently on vacation in Tanzania. Thanks, Idi.

The city of Kampala is a modern clean place. The people speak softly and are overly polite. Oh, there is a war going on, actually three wars. But you would never know it from the ambience of Kampala. There are upscale tourists here, eager to spot gorillas in the south. There are fishermen eager to catch giant Nile perch in the west, and jaded safarists heading to the nearly empty parks. All that Kenya had, Uganda has now. Even the Asians have come back and you can see their kids driving hopped-up European cars and wearing the latest sunglasses. You might think this was Beverly Hills if it wasn't for the giant marabou storks perched on building tops.

After walking back from the museum I have a gin and tonic in the street-level bar outside of the Speke Hotel. The Indian owners are renovating but it still has the creaky atmosphere of an ancient African safari hotel. The veranda is by far the best place to sit and view the park that surrounds the Sheraton. I sit and idly watch the traffic go by. I have to catch a bus that leaves at four in the morning from the bus terminal and I haven't quite figured out how I will entertain myself for the next few hours. The sun goes down. I have been traveling with my friend Rob, a former captain in the Green Berets, now a war correspondent who once enjoyed a closer relationship to war. Now I wonder where he is and head upstairs to our room, about twenty yards away on the first floor.

At 9:30 P.M. a bomb goes off outside our hotel. Rob rolls to the floor and I jump up and grab my camera. Out on the street, at the exact same table where I had been sitting, there is nothing. At first I don't see any victims, then a pool of blood creeps from behind a column toward the street. The explosion has ripped apart three people and injured a few more. My waitress is staring at her white shinbones sticking through her dark legs. There is no moaning or screaming. Just the deathly quiet sound of shock.

Rob jumps into action and tries to help the people, using table-cloths to stanch the blood loss, keeping the worst injured from drifting into death. He screams at the spectators and hotel staff to lend a hand. They watch, frozen. I help to lift the shattered people onto the back of pickup trucks. People stare bug-eyed at our efforts.

It is hard to tell if this is an attack on the hotel, on these specific people, or on tourists. At the moment it's not worth trying to figure out what happened, we're just trying to save lives. The locals continue to stare and then, when one man runs, they all run away like a school of nervous fish.

My hands and camera are slippery from the blood. I am torn between filming, helping, and organizing, so I try to do all three at the same time. We put one man in a chair and I can't help but notice that he has a grasshopper sitting tenaciously on his head through the entire ordeal.

At 11:20 we hear another bomb go off. At first I think it is in the Sheraton up the hill. I jump in the back of the private security truck and we go to the scene. It is not the hotel but a local restaurant, the Nile Grill. Once again there are a few terrified people staring into the darkness behind the restaurant. Apparently three waitresses found a bag in the restaurant and took it to the back to see what was inside. The darkness hides some of the horror.

I gather people and we gently slide blankets under victims. Bones have been pulverized. Legs and arms bend backward in sickening positions. I feel anger. I want the man who put the bomb here to see this, to hear the girls' incoherent mumbling, to try to match the body parts to the right person. As we lift one woman into the back of the pickup truck, I send someone back with a blanket to retrieve her legs.

Rob returns in a rage from the hospital. The doctors and help just sit around and watch. He offered to operate, which almost started a fistfight.

The police have yet to appear at either scene. When they do, they accuse me of being involved since I was the only person who appeared at both explosions. I catch a 4:30 A.M. bus to the front lines in Sudan.

THE WAITING TO GO UP

Yei, New Sudan · A large part of warfare is waiting. You can't just go anywhere you please. Someone has to find petrol for the battered truck. Commanders have to be reached and notified. Preparations have to be made for my arrival. Uniforms scrounged, troops briefed, and so on.

I get used to being bombed. I can even predict the arrival of the evening Antonov, usually a few minutes after the BBC Africa starts. I adopt a tiny goat who wanders around the compound, make friends with the gunmen who guard me, and enjoy the slow laziness of the harsh heat.

Lunch is served at 2:30 P.M. and the interim government walk from their offices and homes to meet at the commish's house. Then one day the cook tells me we will have goat for lunch. My little friend is now smashed into bite-sized bits and covered with flies. At lunch I learn that his intestines have been carefully tied into knots and turned into stew along with the rest of his vitals.

Our exec administrator friend wants to know where our whiskey is. "All Americans have whiskey," he protests when he finds out I don't have any. He tells us that it is very good that we stayed for lunch because the women killed and cooked the goat just for me. We talk about his favorite foods. He doesn't eat goat but he likes cow, mutton, and chicken, animals that do not exist here. His favorite food? Bush rat. A large rodent they catch once in a while that he swears tastes just like chicken. The next time someone asks me what chicken tastes like I'll say bush rat.

I go for a walk among the small collection of huts. An old man wants to show me the bullet holes in his grass roof. Then he shows me his little hand-dug bomb shelter and how he crouches down when they drop bombs. He talks so softly I can barely hear what he is saying.

A few huts over I see a perfectly round hole in the ground. A woman walks up to me and says very shyly and flatly, "Excuse me, sir, can I talk to you? The Antonov bomber came here and dropped bombs on my house and killed my husband and small child." Her remaining child holds up a jagged piece of shrapnel to add to her story.

"Please, sir, what should I do?"

I don't have the answer yet.

THE LIGHT

New York, New York · I don't have any control over how people treat me but there is something that has kept me alive. They tell me it's my eyes. Intimidated at first by a hulking, lurching frame and arrogant demeanor, they say it is my eyes they remember. There is a reason why the Taliban throw stones at my traveling companion and not at me. Why soldiers let me pass and stop others. Why, marked for death in Africa, I got up before the bomb exploded. It's the same look I had when I returned from canoe trips. Open, nonjudgmental, and chillingly focused. It is with these eyes that I recognize others. Other adventurists who seek acceptance and reason. I have seen the same look in many places. In people who are driven by an engine they cannot explain. It is a bond that cannot be broken, a force that defies common sense and rational purpose. I have seen that look in the eyes of hit men, warlords, rebels, commanders, aid workers, and children. I have seen it in the portraits of little-understood men who fade in the pages of history. I do not see that look in the eyes of politicians, priests, or police. It is in the eyes of misfits, people who have chosen their own way to live their lives.

AFGHAN STYLE

Kabul, Afghanistan · I am back in Afghanistan to meet the Taliban again. The fighters want to fire off some rockets for us. Rather than use the beat-up, truck-mounted rocket launcher behind me, they want to show me how they fire rockets mujahideen style, the way they used to back in the days when America supplied mules to carry the rockets up the mountain and the mujahideen didn't have pickup trucks to launch from. To do this the young man and the old man knock the cap well off the bottom of the rocket with a rock, using a messy stack of unexploded rockets as a workbench. They use a fuse instead of an electrical detonator. Dashing off to the side of the road, the older man sets up a crude launching platform made of rocks. The rocks tilt and aim the three-foot rocket in the general direction of the enemy. They then lay stones on top and attach a fuse. They light the fuse and run away. They encourage me to come closer and then, realizing how close I am, warn me back. Too late. The rocket makes a whirring sound and then howls toward the enemy lines. I am sprayed with rocks and pieces of exploded dirt. Close, very close. This type of warfare reminds me of kids playing war except that they are using Soviet-era weapons of great destruction. There doesn't seem to be any shortage of ammunition and one fighter estimates that in one day they go through half a truckload of rockets.

The pace of this war is slow. There are plenty more battles to fight. Back with the fighters is a man who has lost a leg to land mines. His job is to handle supplies and payment. He asks if he can have my small computer because he keeps getting what he pays the fighters wrong.

On the way back from the front lines a fragment of my existence keeps replaying in my head. Between shellfire on the exposed stony ridge, I asked the mullah why the fighters didn't dig trenches or seek shelter from the bombardment. My dark-eyed friend gave me a quizzical look and said, "If you didn't come here to die, then why are you here?"

ACROSS THE
HINDU KUSH

Kabul, Afghanistan · Aristotle, in his teachings to Alexander, said that if he stood on the top of the Hindu Kush he could see the end of the world. He was right. The Persian peoples are the original Aryans, the light-skinned fair-haired peoples that populated Europe and provided the stock for most of America and Europe. They have a long tradition of culture and aesthetics in social, moral, and artistic endeavors. They also war.

At the border on the Khyber Pass the Afghans tell me I missed the execution last Friday, the traditional day of prayers and punishment in Afghanistan. Over 35,000 people gathered in Kabul's national stadium to watch the killing of Bahram for the killing of Asadullah. The father and the brother of the killer pleaded with the Taliban chief justice to spare his life. It was not.

As is the custom here, the family of the victim has the right to shoot the murderer or to forgive him. The family chose *qisas*, or revenge. The victim's brother picked up an AK-47 and shot the man twice while sitting on the back of a red Toyota Hilux pickup truck.

The execution was the second one this year and the eighth in eighteen months of Taliban rule in Kabul. Things have changed since I was here two years ago. Back then the Talibs ringed Kabul, while Massoud, Dostum, and Hekmatyar obliterated the capital with rockets and artillery.

Across the border I must find transportation to Kabul along the most historic and deadly road in Afghanistan. The Khyber Pass. The road follows the Kabul River, eventually begins to climb, and finally gasps for breath as it switches back and forth, winding to the high altitude of Kabul.

The two pimply-faced Taliban guards at the border are not much older than the kids they hit with their metal whips, chain wrapped with colored electrical tape, sort of like flyswatters for humans. One of the smiling Taliban nonchalantly smacks an urchin or two while talking to us. They don't speak a word of English and we speak less Dari, so we shake hands and try to avoid the funky fumes that come from behind their scum-coated teeth. The Taliban are not big on hygiene and they have an unnerving habit of standing very close and staring at you like you are a wax dummy. They also like to stick their heads inside cars like deer at a drive-through zoo. I always wonder how many people get home and find black Taliban turbans caught in their rolled-up windows.

Once over the border I feel a little naked. The last time, we had a shiny Toyota expat mobile, an aging wise driver, and a big, hulking Afghan named Sultan to do all the administrative work. Now I am just a very first-world dufus looking for a cab. If there is one.

I say hello to everyone and hear an English hello back. A young man is traveling to his village on the road to Kabul and I offer to give him a free ride in exchange for negotiating a cab.

While I am talking and walking with my new friend, I walk right by the border post and a man runs out and drags me back. The Talib inside wants to give us a gunman to Kabul and wants us to hire a bus for a usurious $200. I smile and laugh at whatever they say and call them bandits under my breath. I ask, "Is there peace in Afghanistan?" and the man says not yet. I don't know if he is referencing the gunfire outside or predicting what will happen to us on the way to Kabul.

Then I say, "Then there is no crime except for the rates taxi drivers charge." The joke is not missed. I tell him that we will get our own cab, which turns out to be a battered yellow Toyota Corolla for 800,000 Afghanis, or about $22, for the 224-kilometer ride to Kabul. Not bad considering our cab happens to be the last and only cab available this late in the day.

This trip is more interesting because nobody is busy explaining what I am looking at. The area is famous for its Buddhist caves and stupas and was a major center for the Buddhist religion. On my last trip whenever I asked Sultan what I was looking at, he said something like, "Yes, these are things that people have made in the cliffs, maybe some sheep they live there, it is far away, you know these things, you call them caves?" I realize how much knowledge has been lost in Afghanistan.

THE FRONT LINES

Khanabad, Afghanistan · These days the front lines are about eighteen miles west of Taloqan but there are many front lines in Afghanistan. The drive there is through soft green and tan wheat fields. Gentle green hills are patchworked with different colors. The only clue that we have entered a war zone is when we stop for the commander to explain the various front lines that have traded hands over the last few months.

The commander is from Farkhar province, so when we cross into the next province, I ask him if he is homesick. He nods. At a rocket battery and howitzer emplacement he stops to pray.

In an odd use of armament a bridge is blocked by a barrier of light blue five-hundred-pound bombs. The bombs will be used to blow up the bridge if the Talibs advance. Just on the other side is a notch where the road passes through a ridge. This is a dangerous spot. The Talibs can see every vehicle that passes here. The asphalt road has spall marks where the tank shells have hit. They are very recent. My driver stalls and car and I have more time than I want to count the impact marks on the road. Finally he turns left onto a dusty rutted road that winds behind the mass of yellow grass hills. The hills are steep and our new GAZ jeep grinds up the makeshift roads like a metal donkey.

The commander wants to know which outpost I would like to see. I really don't know how one defines which command post is the best one to visit. There is the muffled boom and thunder of war as the weak vehicle screams up the hills, leaving a very large, very easy-to-spot dust plume behind. The artillery shells howl overhead, fired from more than a mile back. I have to get out and walk.

At the top of the hill is a typical Afghan gun emplacement. About twelve fighters are sitting around.

The second position has more men and even a kitchen. It provides a commanding view of the valley and village in the distance. The sun is glinting off the winding river and the Talib tanks are clearly visible. The commander and I stand up in the forward trench and pick out the positions. There are small groups of Alliance men on the crest of the hill before and below us. As the foothills of the mountains start to flatten out, there are Talib positions on the flat plateau. The commander doesn't actually want to destroy these tanks. He wants to capture them, since he lost all his armor when the Talibs took Taloqan.

As is normal on the front lines there is a sense of lazy, frozen time interrupted by howling shells or return fire. The older men run the dashikas and heavy weapons while the younger men must be content to cradle their AKs and watch the show.

The sun is sinking, creating an unearthly golden glow over the yellow grass and on the tanned faces of the fighters. The cook is preparing beans for dinner. We are invited to have tea and biscuits and it is apparent that the fighters are at home here but are not as dull and hardened as the Talibs I met in the south.

On the drive home I pull a new driver. He is reluctant to drive down the steep temporary trails and almost rolls the vehicle twice. I guess from his odd demeanor that he is a hash smoker and is stoned. Tank shells slam into the hill over the crest and herdsmen push their flock toward the river completely oblivious to the shelling and the hidden land mines. After our driver almost rolls the vehicle again I decide to drive. I don't really have time to die in a car accident. The driver sulks and, remembering Afghan pride and revenge, I decide to let him drive part of the way home.

When we get to the pavement, I stop to let him back in the driver's seat. I have made a big mistake. It is the same spot with the splatter marks. I feel like I am in a bad Hollywood thriller as I examine spall marks on the hard pavement while the driver tries to get the vehicle to start. Finally it does and we lead-foot it toward Taloqan.

The drive back is bumpy and dusty as our stoned driver has decided to race a crew in a chopped-top jeep modified to be a mobile rocket launcher. The windshield has been removed and the jeep is crammed full of squinting, hunched-down fighters. I should be thinking about something dramatic but it reminds me of the Beverly Hillbillies' vehicle except we are side by side ready to fly off the road in a heavily mined area.

I pine for the safety and quiet of the front lines.

WAITING

Taloqan, Afghanistan · In between visiting the front lines and interviewing there is much time for nothing. I get used to the Afghan pace of life. The man in the market who lifted up his donkey's ass for me to photograph now makes the same motion every day and laughs uproariously. We are fast friends even though I don't understand a word he says. The kids that follow me around are now known by name to me. The various commanders and fighters have all invited me to tea in their compounds. I am the local celebrity. But I feel that I am more. I am someone who is paying attention to the plight of these people. Someone who will communicate their conditions and opinions to the outside world so far away.

There is much to like about being here. My favorite time is dusk, when the dust from the donkeys floats in the air and paints pastel shadows against the soft colors. Taloqan is dreamlike. The golden sun silhouettes the ancient profiles of turbaned men and ghostlike women gliding in their *burqas*. The line between the gray road and the dust appears to make the people float. Am I seeing the past or the future? Dinners are served, commanders visit, conversation is intense. Hospitality is paramount. There is something here.

THE FLIGHT

Panjshir, Afghanistan · Something is not right. The helicopter can barely budge. The pilot rolls forward on the runway, both engines screaming, and then stops. Then we charge again. We are trying to take off like an airplane but it is not working.

I finally have a ride into Massoud's valley, the Panjshir. There is a crowd assembled around the helicopter. The pilot is yelling at some fighters to get off. The men are wounded and disembark painfully. Then the man who drove them to the airfield forces them back on the plane at gunpoint. I take advantage of the confusion to get back on the chopper. It's not easy to get in. There is a dead body blocking the way. He is in a coffin covered with a green flag, on top of a stack of RPG rocket ammunition in white sacks, thousands of pounds of high explosives. I step gingerly on the rockets as I make my way to the back.

I can hear the yelling outside the window. After much waving of guns and shoving, the pilot gives up. Three men who were accompanying their dead *shahid* (martyr) are put back on. In a funk the pilot turns to the crammed passengers and fighters and shouts. I think he is saying something like "Buckle up and no cell phones." Haneef, our translator, tells me that he said, "If you want to burn, then we will all burn together!" He slams the thin door to the cockpit and the engine revs up.

The Hind helicopter tilts forward at a sickening angle, putting all the weight on the front tires. No lift. Tucked behind the yellow fuel tank, I realize I am in for the hairiest or last ride of my life. At the end of the runway the pilot pushes the blades even farther forward and we are surrounded in dust. I look out the window. We are flying. Barely.

We skim and clip treetops. Green hilltops brush by the worn-out wheels. The pilot avoids high hills by flying through the valleys. I don't know if we are staying low to avoid the Talib jets or if we just can't climb any higher. An image is burned into my mind: an old man on a donkey sitting on a hilltop looking down on us with wide eyes.

As we get off in the Panjshir, my cameraman, Peter, asks me if I saw the blood oozing out of the coffin onto the polished aluminum floor. I really wasn't paying attention.

THE LION

Taloqan, Afghanistan · "You are late for maneuvers. Please hurry," says the military messenger who shows up along the road. "Please hurry, Massoud will be there," he entreats us.

Our driver hurries the best he can. He had his hand blown up when defusing a land mine. Our bodyguard has some deep scars where bullets ripped through him. He winces when we hit a bump. The lead is still embedded inside him. Even Peter complains about the shrapnel that comes out of his leg every once in a while.

Arriving at the flat plains east of Taloqan in the blue twilight, I can see fire spitting from a heavy gun. Massoud is trying out some new weapons. They are firing over our jeep into the mountains above us. The idea is right out of *Mad Max* and *The Rat Patrol*. They have taken the tops off some new Russian-made GAZ jeeps and mounted a heavy DShK 12.7mm and a KPVT 14.5mm. Massoud is easy to spot. He has a backwash of about eighty people who follow him in a tightly knit pack. When he stops to look through his binoculars, they stop. When he walks, they walk. It is almost as if standing néxt to him will impart some benefit or at least temporary celebrity.

Massoud loves toys. He has a Hummer sitting under a tarp in the Panjshir, Scud missile launchers, and even two Hind gunships outside his house. Although car-mounted weapons aren't new in other wars, these are the latest in the evolution of warfare in Afghanistan.

Throughout it all Massoud is very much the man in charge, shouting out orders to adjust this, try that, do it again, and whatever. He points, looks through binoculars, using great gesticulation when he speaks. He is the commander. The role model for a generation of fighters in Afghanistan. He has changed from the Banana Republic waistcoat or field jacket to a sporty yachting-slash-hunting-jacket look.

When he sees me, he gives me a quick sly nod and continues his starring role. He is very aware of the cameras and, had I not seen the stock footage from the last ten years, I would not have noticed that he plays to the camera in pacing and positioning. Even the idea of blasting dashikas and mortaring hillsides seems camera perfect. It is an Afghan version of a sound and light show.

The next day Massoud invites us to do our interview. We are taken to a secret location surprisingly close to where the bombs were dropped last week. He is sitting alone, perfectly framed through the fruit trees, reading a book on the porch of a large house. He is called the Lion of the Panjshir and with this angle you can almost hear the voice-over.

Up close he has a striking face, a large hook nose and almond eyes that almost look like they have been enhanced with eyeliner. He wears a trademark wool hat that he first adopted when he began his fight in mountainous Nuristan. Now all his fighters have adopted the hot wool hat. The jaunty rake of his *pakool* has become a caricature of himself. But he is the real thing, one of the few men on this earth who are willing to fight for a principle and do not let power corrupt them. It is only because he has steadfastly maintained this outward image that he appears to be a caricature. Unchangeable, pure, and driven, he is immune to the passage of time or political fashion.

Nevertheless you can't help feeling in his presence that he is also a good actor, gracious, fluid, seasoned, and matured in his tedious role. His words are carefully chosen and elegantly communicated. His eyes flash, his smile engages, his demeanor is lordlike. But in this play there is no understudy and his audience is drifting away; the tragedy has run too long. It seems that his precocious and now formulaic talent for war fighting does not resonate with the outside world. Like any great actor who is slightly past his prime, should he retire or remake himself to suit the realities of the new geopolitical situation? A world where wars are won in boardrooms, through shuttle diplomacy, in newspapers, and in tedious political meetings.

His Western supporters describe him as the Che Guevara of our times, the Ho Chi Minh of Afghanistan. And then, remembering that America does not embrace these icons, they will add "the George Washington of Afghanistan." The Taliban describe Massoud as a war criminal, a man who would be hung from the nearest tall object like Najibullah, who swung for days from a traffic post with coins, cigarettes, and money stuffed in his mouth. The sign of a puppet.

In Massoud's territory there are none who could be considered detractors. Massoud is the miracle worker, defeater of the Russians, virtuous, kind, respectful, and brilliant. A destroyer of enemies as well as a builder of cities and armies. People's eyes light up when they describe Massoud. Massoud shrugs off this adulation. Although he is a man who has elevated himself so highly in the minds of his people that there would be catastrophic shock should he fall ill or die, he doesn't see himself as a leader.

I am doing an interview even though I am not a journalist and I can't imagine what I will do with the pat political answers he provides. His latest thing is railing against the Taliban as puppets of Pakistan. This isn't true, based on my firsthand experience, and I take a little time to argue the point. The Talibs are no more puppets of Afghanistan than he is a puppet of Iran, a country that provides weapons and money in an effort to distract the Talibs from the south. I don't get into the fact that Massoud has now aligned himself with the Russians through Tajikistan, a sensitive subject that says more about Massoud's pragmatism than his political position.

When faced with these criticisms, most friends will say Massoud is Massoud. He is also a xenophobe, an upper-class Tajik who has traveled very little, distrusts outside support, is immensely practical and creative, a singular authoritarian who handles details personally. So much so that almost every major decision is run by him for his okay or modification. A man who courts the press but does not care what they say. A man who by birth, violent circumstances, and outside forces has become the last hope of the Afghan people for peace yet who insists that the Afghan people will choose who will lead them once the peace is won.

People who have known him for the last ten or twenty years will tell you that there is a difference in Massoud. He is more tired now. He has outlived most of his friends and commanders. He has seen his area of influence shrink to less than 10 percent of Afghanistan and in reality he controls only the forbidding mountains the southern Talibs are so reticent in taking. Before the Talibs, he had a small war coordinating tight-knit groups of commanders. Now he has Machiavellian nightmares as commanders switch sides and outside forces shift or fade away. He is fighting on three fronts and with an army that is no longer using guerrilla tactics but is defending fixed positions with sparse weaponry. He draws a map to show me the front lines and I am surprised to see it become a circle. He is immensely confident that even though he may not win, he will not lose. He faced his toughest hour when the Talibs overran Taloqan and pushed them into the mountains. He may have even been happiest as they lured the Talibs up the steep hills, ambushed them, lured them up again, and killed some more. When the southern lowland Talibs began throwing up and fainting from the effects of altitude, they killed some more. He smiles. No one will shake him from his mountains.

HOMEWARD

Taloqan, Afghanistan · This is the day we are supposed to leave. Laundry has been rotated, aired, and reused. Cameras are dusty and dinged and we are running out of most things. Breakfasts are shrinking down to a few raisins, dusty off-color cheese, and stale bread. Like sex, love, and food, each trip has its natural rhythm. The exuberant beginning, the explosion of new sounds, sights, and smells, and the slow descent into routine and dullness. It is time to go.

To stay longer would also mean dipping into other things. People, events, and cataclysms that might blur the sharp focus of my purpose. I find that if you stay too long you start to accept many of the things you once thought strange. You lose your objectivity, like doing an autopsy on your own children.

THE MENTOR

Las Vegas, Nevada · Krott gives me the heads-up. "There's a journalist here from New York, Canadian. She's bought your book, wants to meet you." Krott can be counted on to show up at the Soldier of Fortune Convention every year. Ex–Green Beret captain: official things in Korea, Somalia, vague things in Bosnia, Sudan, and Central America. Writer and mellow travel companion. The fall event has become a regular time to get together. We look out for each other, meet like-minded people, make fun of the crowd, promise not to come back, and show up every year.

Krott's quick heads-up and briefing was a courtesy sitrep designed to give me time to lock and load. I like the military's xenophobic approach to outsiders. I should be the ultimate outsider in a room full of mercs, feds, ex-mil, marines, Vietnam vets, and others. Yet here I am a respected insider. Maybe it's a guy thing, maybe it's because I know how to tune the engine beneath the tough-guy veneer. Every year I meet people here I just couldn't meet anywhere else. Good ol' boys who train the DEA, high and tight SpecFors who provide medical care for refugees, a lot of ex-military trying to get that feeling, when life was good and terribly short. I tell people I come here to sign books but it's really about meeting kindred souls. Men and women who seek adventure for its own sake.

I am already forming an image of the kind of female journo who would waste time at SOF: kinky stiff hair, loose flowered dress, battered notebook, third-world bag that doubles as a purse, and a cheerful but ceramic interest toward people who would be found at events like this. She's here for the cartoon side of gun love, man love, cammo, and swagger. She'll get plenty of it. We'll just point Carl the faux legionnaire out to her, take her over to the booth where they sell Nazi marching songs, steer her to rotund men who warn of the New World Order, have her buy a few manuals on how to kill people, blow things up, and live in the woods. She'll get her story but without me in it. Journalists are only here for guns and bellies. I don't want to get caught in the cross fire.

The opening cocktail party at the twentieth annual Soldier of Fortune Convention wasn't much. Never is. A pathetic attempt at adding ceremony to middle-aged men who have nowhere else to hang out. Publisher Robert K. Brown, now deaf as a post from years of gunshots, is admiring a gold-plated Colt .45 with his engraved likeness on the white plastic grips. "I sure was a handsome fucker," he cackles. It will be auctioned to help men who go behind enemy lines to provide medical care when no one else dares to go. They won't be in any article because they don't give a shit. For them it's about doing good and having a good time. The rest of the auction money will go to pay Brown's legal bills. Back when *SOF* was really about and for mercs he got screwed when someone used the classifieds in the back of the magazine to hire a hit man, the equivalent of suing NBC because you saw a war movie and punched your neighbor. Typical bullshit. Tonight, though, Brown is in his element, a man among his men, Nam vets who hung out in Salvador, went hunting in Africa, and have rubbed enough of the dirty world on them to think they are mercs. It's not surprising that on Brown's leg cast the biggest signature just says "Fuck You."

By the time Sarah the journalist makes her entrance a crew has begun to form around the portable bar with four-dollar beers. My first guess is Vancouver, liberal arts, by the hairstyle and no makeup. Her clothes are an odd blend of teenager and yuppie. Athlete, student, and maybe even eighties disco. Go figure. Chalk it up to owning a mishmash of old clothes or not giving a shit. Tall, thin, elegant, she hovers between twenty-five and forty-five depending on how the light catches her. Most of the time the light catches her around thirty. She talks young but walks old. Either way, any way, I am intrigued.

She, however, doesn't seem to give a damn about who I am. This is good and this is bad. Krott had made a space next to me but she dropped her stuff and kept going, started talking to someone else. I'll have to talk to Krott about his briefings.

Sarah spends the next few minutes standing a bit too close and staring too intently into the person's face while they talk. You don't do that with men that age. It makes them nervous.

Coming back, she acts like she forgot who I was. Good training, take the first punch and then come back when they are off balance.

She would have gotten away with it if it wasn't for her eyes. I have to watch out for this girl. She wants something.

Sarah is twenty-six, intense, stares directly at me with blue eyes that never waver. She answers with pauses preceded by an "umm" or "weeell," as if the extra space buys her time to formulate or perhaps create an answer. She used to be a journalist at some podunk rag in Canada but now she is a fact-checker for KPMG. She works when she can at magazines like *Men's Journal* and the *New Yorker*. Like playing Russian roulette, she says: miss one mistake out of thousands of facts and you're gone. She has also worked for some writers fact-checking their books or articles. Adventure writers, she says—not quite like you, though. I smile. I think she can tell what I think about the cocktail-adventure genre. At first I want to scrape away her New York sense of self-importance but then I find myself feeling protective. I recognize something about her. This is a person from the same places I am. She has guts.

Sarah told me later that she thought I would talk to her for two minutes and then blow her off. She was surprised that I asked her questions about herself. I saw the fear of rejection in her eyes, the horror that someone would ask a few questions and then turn her out.

She thought the show would make a good article and she wants to pitch it around town. Either the worst cover story for an investigative reporter or a badly shaped alibi for a weekend in Vegas. I get the unnerving feeling that she didn't come to find something in Las Vegas, she is running away from something in New York.

She mentions that in my book I say I went to St. John's. Her family bought the meat we sold door-to-door from me. I quickly do the math. Eighteen years between us. She is young enough to be my daughter. I am young enough not to notice. We talk a bit about my youth as if it means something to her. As she talked and I talked, I sensed both rejection and a plea for help, over her head and in her element. I am hooked. This is going to be an interesting weekend.

The SOF show was dull, as all of them are. Large men selling machine guns, bored married women sitting behind dirty glass cases. Lots of black golf shirts from sales reps mixed in with faded cammo. Exhibitions on knife fighting, water survival, and other useless skills. Here and there an interesting person, a novel business, an old friend.

Throughout it all Sarah spent her time working at the job she doesn't have. I have a chance to watch her from afar. She is rudderless in her interviews, too observant, too caring, and too "I'm just asking questions" to connect with this crowd. She doesn't know it but she has the distinction of being the only person pretending to be a print reporter here. There is a crew from NBC and a gushing German producer with an L.A. pickup crew. Everyone knows that outsiders are bad news here. By the end of the day most have assumed that Sarah is either a harmless tourist or a very good professional. She doesn't push, she doesn't shape, she doesn't even ask the questions you are supposed to ask. Hell, she hardly even takes notes and when she does she writes down everything you say.

At the obligatory pool gathering where the conventioneers break off into clusters, Sarah starts talking to me. Not about the things you are supposed to talk about, but about life, marriage, and adventure. She married an Iranian man about a year ago and now she feels smothered. He is a sensitive guy. His family are rich Iranians who have a big construction company but left for Montreal. Do I ever feel smothered? Have I ever yielded to temptation? I know which answers she wants to hear. And I want to give her those answers. But later, when I ask if her husband would let her go to a place like Chechnya, she says he would but he would cry. She isn't smothered. I don't need to ask her why she married. I know why. I married for the same reason.

We sit together during a banquet. The speaker was a famous adventurer fifteen years ago. Jack Wheeler, a man who has journeyed to dangerous places, shot tigers, swum ocean straits, braved death, even helped create the Reagan doctrine. He starts the speech by asking, "How many men does it take to open a beer? None! It should already be open when she brings it!" The crowd roars at the nonjoke. He protests the "faggotization and feminization" of America. Thunderous applause, standing ovation. He closes by saying "God bless America!," more thunderous applause, longer standing ovation. There is no more to be said to please this crowd.

Everyone cheers. Sarah is shaking her head in disbelief. Gotcha. Her Canadian, liberal, no-makeup soul is showing through. Only girls who want to be like men give a shit what men think. Sarah wants to be like her dad, adventurous, worldwise, and smart. But maybe she can't because she is a beautiful woman. I wonder if she'll believe me when I tell her she can be both. I want to tell her how to be an adventurist. How to bring every skill, every fear, and every passion to life. But what gives me the right?

Right now I need to know if I can trust Sarah. She never did give me a straight answer on why she came here to this place, at this time. She said she read *Soldier of Fortune* magazine when she was young. She has an older brother who is a flight attendant. Something about her father being a tough guy. A pilot—no, the best pilot. She said she was here because she felt she could learn something.

Does she want to learn or is she just a visitor? I point out that she answers each question I ask with a pause. I ask her to just say what she thinks, not what she thinks I want to hear.

The next day Sarah watches the cammo-jacketed men as they diligently shoot machine guns lined up in a row. The shooting range also has little explosive charges on sticks. An old deaf man with a shaved head hobbles around in a uniform with a jungle cap. The man is Peter Kokalis, known as an expert on weapons. He introduces each machine gun and the gunner, and then all two dozen or so machine guns fire at once at the dirt in front of them. It wasn't about hitting anything, it was about the sound.

Sarah wants to interview the old man. Her pad has long been filled up with scribbles, so I offer to get her a new pad and accompany her to the interview. She interviews Kokalis and dutifully writes down what he says. She is really trying hard to be a journalist but she is missing the bolt that locks in the self-confidence you need to do this. The same way I had tried so hard to be a copywriter, lumberjack, tunneler, driller, and marketing guru. But I had had help from people who wanted me to succeed, people long dead and far away.

I was going to help this girl enter a world she never imagined, be a mentor with a protecting hand. I tell her I will be meeting someone who is probably a little more interesting. A mujahideen, but more important an American. We are planning a mission to one of the world's most dangerous places, Chechnya, to rescue a small girl in the middle of a brutal war. Forty thousand Russians have attacked and only two thousand mujahideen remained . . . to die.

At first she thinks I am playing for effect but my eyes tell her to be careful. She laughs. "Like my dad says. It ain't bragging if you can do it." The thing is, no one will know we've done it except three people and a small girl. Journalists don't go where we go or do what we do. We will have to walk through the snowy mountains of Georgia and we may be trapped for months. Would she like a real story, instead of listening to old men go on? Sarah says yes, far too fast. And I let her.

THE MARTYR

Phoenix, Arizona · I had been talking to the gruff-sounding man over the phone for weeks. He used the name Abu Saif, the "father of the sword." He had been told by some military people that I was an okay guy to talk to, a little curt, a little opinionated, but someone to be trusted.

He had told me he was a Muslim, a mujahid, and he had a problem. His wife and daughter were still in Chechnya. Exactly where he didn't know. Could I get him in to find her?

When I first went to visit, I was surprised by the neighborhood he lived in, an a upscale suburb in the south of town. I was surprised again when he walked out to greet me. I had expected an olive-skinned hatchet-faced immigrant. What I saw was a young American, a football-star, young-cop, bull-rider, working-on-the-line kind of man. A young man with a home that was tastefully furnished with drapes, pictures, aquarium, and toys. He had a wife here, three strawberry-blond children, and an AK-47 leaning up against the wall.

Aqil was a bad boy. Born in Hawaii, absent father, he ended up in the California youth camps. In the camps he saw an open Koran, started reading, and liked what he saw. He became a Muslim and when he got out he went to the mosques to pray. There a man who tinted windows told him about jihad, about each Muslim's opportunity to enter paradise by fighting the infidels. Within a few weeks and without any military training he was on his way to Bosnia. After Bosnia he was sent for training to Afghanistan. He had to hide when the Pakistani secret service showed up. He was supposed to go to Tajikistan but that fell through and he was sent to Kashmir. When the Pakistanis saw a young American with a big red beard, they turned him around and sent him home. He fought in Chechnya. Although accepted by the Arabs and other mujahideen, he soon became bored. Looking for action, he found a group of misfits and took up with them. Together they attacked Russian army bases, helicopters, and tanks. The commanders scolded him for bringing so much heat on them. He would sneak across enemy lines to watch kung fu movies in town, wearing grenades strapped to his chest in case he was caught.

His appendix blew. They operated but after two days he put on his pack and started walking, ripping the sutures and bleeding daily. He never really healed completely.

When he traveled around, his Chechen friends would ask village girls if they would marry him. Sight unseen, they would say yes. When asked why, the girls said they would marry a fighter even if he had no legs or arms. Touched by this, he vowed to marry a Chechen girl. He met a beautiful one at a market stall, Ayesha. On his wedding day he was awakened with the news that Russians were invading the village. He ran out half dressed and tripped a Russian Claymore.

Hundreds of ball bearings blew through his legs and he fell. Bandaged and on his way to a field hospital, he begged to be allowed to marry Ayesha. He did and took her to Jordan, where he could recover. Frustrated at having a dead foot, he told the doctors to cut it off.

For a few years he tried to get Ayesha back to the States. Without a job, money, or help it was no go. Finally she left in frustration, taking their daughter to Chechnya.

Back in the United States he heard about me when the CIA handed him a copy of *Dangerous Places* and said, "Here, this will tell you what's going on over there."

He wants me to get him inside Chechnya. The people who smuggle the fighters in have told him to wait. He can't. Russians are bombing and killing civilians. He has to go. Why does he need me? I must bring his wife and daughter back. He will stay, to fight and to die.

My next adventure has begun.

THE ADVENTURIST

Somewhere over the earth · All my trips begin and end with a plane flight, a magical experience that lifts me from the troubles and reality of this life and suspends me in a crystal-blue paradise. As I sweep in great arcing circles, there is much to see that inspires awe. Thunderheads inside clouds, turquoise coral reefs, jagged cliffs, smoke-ribboned volcanoes, arctic snows, red deserts, lights of great cities. A magnificent theater scaling the ego and ambition of its players back to size. Down below, people are dying, laughing, screaming, loving, sleeping, crying. I can't hear them from up here but I can feel them.

There is something about the clarity of altitude that brings insight. Five miles up flying at six hundred miles an hour, I can let my mind take wing. Flying in a time-wasted, fatigued haze, I can reflect on what I have done, who I am, and what I do. I have lived a life driven both inwardly and outwardly. Despite the bruises and the scars, it feels good. And I have much to do.

I am drawn from my comfortable existence into the world's most hellish places like a moth to a flame. Caught between the desire for new adventure and the enveloping warmth of home. But like home, adventure is not places so much as people. When I leave for dangerous places, it is because some Darwinian process seems to have filled these horrific places with only the most driven, the most resolute, people who burn furious but briefly.

Like the tempering of steel or polishing of diamonds, the objects of my interest have been formed into something undeniably intense and valuable. And like Hercules with his tasks, or Odysseus with his journey, I find if I weather the storms I return home with something of value. There is nothing heroic about my vocation; it is what I am driven to do, my pleasure, the fuel that fires my engine. When I return, time slows down. I force myself to enjoy gentle subtleties, to pick up the startling rhythm of clocks, bills, television, and civilization. I decompress, relax, and after the dirt and the horror are washed away, I start to rebuild my energy. And then, as if preordained, a flash of light will catch my eye and I will wander toward it. I am an adventurist and I cannot change that.

I pause when I'm asked, "Is there anywhere you fear going?" But I don't tell them that my greatest fear is not having a place to return to. That I will lose one side of my balancing pole and go reeling off into the darkness below.